To

Ronnie

Brummie to another

OUR BRUM

VOLUME 2

Carl Chinn

all the best

[signature]

ISBN: 0 9534316 0 6

First published 1998 by Birmingham Evening Mail, 28 Colmore Circus, Birmingham B4 6AX.

Typeset, printed and bound in Great Britain by HE Jones Ltd., Birmingham.

CONTENTS
OUR BRUM VOLUME 2

FOREWORD

Whenever Carl Chinn visits the Evening Mail offices, his progression through the newsroom is like that of a benign tornado – a swirling bundle of energy, excitement and enthusiasm.

His Brummie tones ring out as he greets all those in his path with a loud welcome, a pat on the back, an arm round the shoulder. His very presence brings forth smiles from even the most cynical.

When Carl breezed in to ask for permission to reprint some of his best Evening Mail columns in a book a year ago, we readily agreed. 'Our Brum – Part 2' is a second glorious collection of his 'All Our Yesterdays' columns, full of the memories of Birmingham as our great city used to be.

This time there are many photographs which have never previously been published, half of them from the Evening Mail archives and the rest sent in by our readers and reproduced here for the first time. It is not only a fascinating trip back through time, but an invaluable lesson for generations to come. Each of the letters and photographs submitted are copied and placed in a special archive at Birmingham Central Library.

The 'Old Brum' archive now contains more than 20,000 letters ranging from brief memories to full-blown life stories, and more than 6,000 photographic images of the way we were.

Community Historian Carl is a Brummie born and bred, and his writing captures perfectly the passion he feels for his city roots. Long may he continue to delight us all.

Ian Dowell
Editor
Birmingham Evening Mail

BRUMMIES

BACK-TO-BACK SMILES

A throng of short streets strikes out from the main drag. Each has a different name, but all of them are the same. They are dark, noisy and pungent. Smoke belches out of countless chimneys, sounds clamour from every direction and smells waft upwards from innumerable buildings. There is so little space and yet so many people pour into such a small area. They've been pulled in by industry and they're held fast by work, familiarity, neighbours and kin. Some of them live in front and back houses - they've got two rooms downstairs - but most crowd into the hundreds and hundreds of back-to-backs.

They were built by speculative builders who crammed as many dwellings as they could into as small an area as was possible. Most were constructed badly by jerry-builders who were looking for a short-term profit. They used dirt instead of sand for the mortar and they covered the walls with thin

Look at the spotless pinnies on the woman and child standing on the scrubbed doorstep of their back house in 15 Court, Adams Street, Duddeston, about 1905. This was one of the poorest streets in Brum, yet like so many others this woman has not given in to the dirt and smoke all around. She shouts out her pride not only through well washed clothes but also through clean curtains and nets on her windows. The entry to the yard can just be seen to the left, behind the gas lamp hanging from the wall. On the right, close to the clothes line pole, is a maiding tub, used for washing.

(Thanks to Birmingham Library Services, 'Slum Collection')

Ford Street, Hockley in the late 1950s or early 1960s. A typical Birmingham back street with kids playing along the horse road and houses and businesses cheek-by-jowl. On the right are the premises of George Barton, pawnbroker, distinctive with three brass balls hanging from the wall. Going down that side are Karmo Developments, motor cycle accessory manufacturers; Wasdell Thomas, mudguard makers; and Lloyd, Pascall and Co, fancy brassware manufacturers. Is that the factory of Rabone's, the rule makers at the end of the street – and at the bottom is that the bus garage in Whitmore Street? (Thanks to James Dixon)

lathes, horse's hair and plaster. It's not surprising that stinking bugs, slithery silver fish, vile black bats and other foul vermin infest the houses - no matter how hard the women graft to keep them clean. And when a new babby is born, the crib is made up from one of the drawers, or else from an orange box from the local greengrocer.

Downstairs, there's a pokey scullery filled with just a sink and a couple of shelves, and there's one main room. This does for almost everything. With the big black range, it's a kitchen. With a table and chairs, it's a dining room. And with its squab, it's a living room. For mothers it's also a work room. Here they iron and clean. If they're poor, it's here that they work on carding buttons and hooks and eyes, at chopping up and bundling firewood, and at a multitude of other hard and weary tasks to stave off hunger.

Some back-to-backs front on to the street itself, but most are approached up a tight and low entry which leads into a yard. This has a number of communal facilities; there's a brew'us in which the women do the washing; there's the miskins where the rubbish is put; there are two or three lavatories shared between six or more families. And, until the late 1930s, there's a tap which supplies water for all the folk who live in the yard.

Strangers shrink from the areas which are packed with back-to-backs. They see them as dreary places, rocking with noises and polluted by the whiff of gas, steam and horse manure. They're right. The outlook is gloomy. It's loud and the atmosphere is filled with stenches. But they miss something. Here, where the environment is so hostile, there are people bonding together, Here where there are slums, there are neighbourhoods.

No-one can mourn the destruction of insanitary, decrepit back-to-backs. But in sweeping away the back-to-backs, we failed to see the kids who played safely on the streets, the women who laid out the dead, who brought babies into the world and who had remedies. The back-to-backs of Brum may have gone - but the Brummies who lived in them still have something to teach us about living together.

Children playing in the yard back of 315-330, Icknield Port Road, Ladywood, early 1960s. The front houses are near to the junction with Freeth Street and not far from the 'Crown' Picture House. On the right are the communal lavatories and behind them are the brew'uses – wash-houses. The back-to-backs in this photo seem to have been renovated by the council, indicating that they would not be knocked down until the late 1960s and emphasising the widespread nature of bad housing inherited from the nineteenth century. In a clear connection with the Adams Street photo, notice the cleanliness of the children, the nets and curtains – marks of respectability achieved in spite both of poverty and the inadequate facilities locally. (Thanks to Johnny Landon)

HEART OF THE COUNTRY:
RURAL BRUM

Brum is one of the great cities of Europe. It's a boisterous, clamorous, rumbustious place. Factories, shops, offices and houses cover the land. Roads, railway lines and canals abound. And there are people everywhere. There seems to be no trace of our city's agricultural past.

It's as if everything rural has been banished and forgotten in the name of progress.

But think again! In the midst of this huge urban space there are constant reminders of the countryside. Just take a stroll along the Cole Valley Walkway. Start at the Dingles, carry on through Springfield, Greet and Hay Mills and before you know it, you're in Sheldon. Apart from when you cross a few main roads, you'd never imagine you were in one of the most populous parts of England. Following the river, stepping through long grass in the shadow of numerous trees, watching out for foxes and voles, harking to a multitude of birds - you'd swear you were deep in the heart of the country.

And when you go shopping, how many of us still say we're going "down the village?" There's

John Izod and his family outside Grove Farm Farm, Sparkhill, 1895. Within a few years the farm was to disappear and its fields were to be covered with Grove Road, Greswolde Road and Nansen Road. Although officially part of Sparkhill, many of us grew up knowing this neighbourhood as Springfield. (Birmingham Library Services: photo taken by Mrs Fanny H. Walker of 58, Camp Hill)

Moseley Village, Kings Heath Village, Erdington Village, Acocks Green Village and Ward End Village - just to name a few. Today all of these are bustling and busy, but there are still tranquil sites in Brum which have the feel of a village, like Kings Norton with its Green, St Edburgha's in Yardley and St Laurence's in Northfield.

Then there's all street names which recall quieter and calmer times - and they're not just to be found on the outskirts of Birmingham. You can't get much nearer to the middle of the city than Bull Street, Cherry Street, Moat Lane or Windmill Street by the Horse Fair. And let's not forget Summer Lane, Heath Street in Winson Green, Wood Lane in Handsworth, Farm Street in Hockley, Green Lane in Small Heath, and Willows Crescent in Balsall Heath. What of Coneybere Street in Highgate? It's the place where the rabbits (coneys) once ran in the barley (bere).

Buildings also shout out the significance of old Brum's rural heritage. There's so many of them, if only we'd just take notice. Pop in to St Martin's in the Bull Ring - erected when Brummagem was just a small market town. See Blakesley Hall in Yardley, constructed in the late1500s by Richard Smallbrooke. There's Cole Hall in Shard End, Selly Manor in Bournville, Stratford House at Camp Hill, and St Peter's Church in Harborne.

It's May Day 1910 and Harry Holt, a carter, from Wythall is holding the horse's head at Titterford Farm, Yardley Wood. When Birmingham City Council took over Titterford Mill and Pond it changed the tame to Trittiford to avoid potential embarassment from the original spelling.

Gathering the hay at Ashold Farm, Tyburn in 1915. On the photo are John Scott Rumble, Ted Rumble, Reg Rumble, Joe Kelly, Al Tidmarsh and Harry Bourn. Much of the land was used as a sewage farm. The Rumbles still have a business locally, a cafe by the Tyburn House. (Thanks to Howard Rumble)

Right by the Outer Circle 11 route in Hall Green, there's Sarehole Mill, which used to be owned by the Andrews family. Until 1919, they were still milling corn here. Nearby is Moseley Bog. Originally, it was the site of a supplementary storage pool for the mill, but today it's an enchanting wetland where rare plants are found and in which wildlife thrives. In the late 1890s, the world famous author J.R.R. Tolkien lived a few yards away. As a child his imagination was affected deeply by the Mill, the local countryside and its folk. Just read *The Hobbit* and *Lord Of The Rings* if you want to wallow in the influence of rural Brum.

The Andrews weren't the only ones still engaged in agricultural work in Birmingham well into the twentieth century. Farmers, dairymen, pig keepers and others all lived and collared within the city's boundaries. It was the presence of large farms which allowed the council to build 50,000 municipal houses in the inter-war years - the largest number constructed by any authority in Western Europe.

Think of some of the estates where they are to be found. There's Pineapple Farm in Stirchley, Billesley Farm, Stonehouse Farm in California. There's Glebe Farm, Batchelors Farm in Little Bromwich, Trittiford Farm in Yardley Wood and Allen's Cross Farm in Northfield.

The fields and animals may have gone from here and elsewhere - but wherever we look, the legacy of old farmland Brum is with us still.

OUR BRAVE HEROES:
THE BIRMINGHAM PALS

It was the highlight of the year for every part-time soldier - the annual camp when they trained with their mates and concentrated just on army matters without having to think of work the next day. Ever since 1870, the territorial battalions of the Royal Warwicks had been going away on this kind of trip. At first they'd only gone to Sutton Coldfield, but gradually they went further and this summer they were off to Rhyl.

They might not have been regulars, but no-one could knock this lot for their commitment, determination and enthusiasm. There was no doubt that they looked a fine sight as they gathered that Sunday morning on August 2nd 1914. With boots polished, buttons glistening and uniforms pressed they trooped off to their trains, led by the regimental band playing the 'Warwickshire Lad'. Yet they'd only been in North Wales for a few hours when they were commanded back to Birmingham. On their

Recruits of the 2nd Birmingham Battalion going along Corporation Street on their way to church parade in St Martin's in the Bull Ring, Sunday 11 October 1915. They are passing Warwick Chambers, now the site of C&A the department store.

(Information from Terry Carter, Birmingham Pals. 14th, 15th and 16th (Service) Battalions of the Royal Warwickshire Regiment. A History of the Three City Battalions Raised in Birmingham in World War One, 1997)

Kitted out soldiers of the 3rd City battalion at camp in Malvern, 1915.

return, their colonel had no further orders, although as he dismissed them, he warned to be ready for a speedy return to barracks as war was looming across Europe.

The call to arms came more quickly than they could have anticipated. Just the next day, August 4th, the Kaiser sent his troops into Belgium even though it was a neutral country and the United Kingdom immediately declared war on Germany. That afternoon at 5.30pm, the mobilisation of the British army began and something quite remarkable happened. It wasn't just a matter of the regulars reporting for duty and making themselves ready. Throughout Britain and Ireland, territorials flocked to do their duty.

In Brum, factory blokes, shop workers and fellers from the corporation left behind their families and rushed to join their pals - and so did small gaffers, shopkeepers and wealthy businessmen. Not one of them wanted to let down their mates. Not one of them wanted to let down their regiment. And not one of them wanted to let down their city.

The 5th battalion of the Royal Warwicks gathered at their base in Thorp Street, the 6th battalion at the Midland Railway Sheds in Suffolk Street and the 8th battalion at their headquarters in Aston, by Witton Island. In only three hours the units were ready. As they set off to Snow Hill there was no rousing music nor were there stirring speeches. None were needed. These part-timers realised the seriousness of the situation and they knew that many of them might never return. But their hearts must have swelled as they marched along the streets of their town. Tens of thousands of Brummies had crowded on to the footpaths of the city centre. There were cheers from knots of men and women as they spotted a mucker or a relative. Mostly there was silence. It wasn't a silence of shame or dislike - it was a deep, powerful silence full of pride and respect. The folk of Brummagem had come to let their lads know one thing - they were with them.

For the first year of the war the 5th, 6th and 8th were stationed in Essex, prepared to defend London in case of a German invasion. Then in March 1915 they boarded boats at Folkestone and

disembarked at Le Havre in France. The ranks of the regular army had been decimated by the vicious fighting on the Western Front and territorials were needed desperately to hold back the enemy. The Brummie battalions were attached to the 48th, the South Midland Division, and after a short time at 'Plug Street' in Belgium they were sent to the Somme.

That winter of 1915 was dreadful. The German trenches were just 400 yards away, but it was so cold and wet that both forces spent most of their time bailing out water from their positions. In the following summer, battle was joined in a most frightening and destructive way. Early in the morning on July 16th 1916, the 6th and 8th battalions of the Royal Warwicks were sent over the top. The sun was bright and the sky was clear as these Brummie blokes scrambled out of their trenches and into the death-trap of No Man's Land. The German machine guns mowed them down and yet those who were left still went forward for King and Country.

In four terrible hours the battalions suffered 588 casualties out of 600 men. Amongst them were 230 dead. With all those killed in the Great War they are remembered in a Roll of Honour in Birmingham's Hall of Memory off Broad Street.

Let's hope that the Brummies of the future forget neither the horror of war nor those men of Old Brum who gave their lives in the belief that there would be no more wars.

William Henry Grice of the Royal Warwickshire Regiment with his daughter Florence May aged ten, 1917. This photo was taken whilst William was recuperating from a leg wound.
(Thanks to Albert Grice)

THE CREAM OF ITALY

Reaching the bend in the road, the little group of half a dozen men and women stopped as if they were moved by the same force. Slowly they turned and looked back along the dirt road to the little town of Gallinaro, gathered on a crest of a hill. They could make out the walls which surrounded the place and their gaze was drawn inwards to the squat structure of the ancient church with its bell tower and cross rising from the road. The piazza was hidden from view but in their imaginations they saw it clearly. Hemmed in by old houses and drawing to it a tangle of tight alleys and tiny streets, the small square had been at the centre of their lives and those of their ancestors since time beyond memory.

Lying in the Comino Valley, high in the mountains of southern Italy, their town and the surrounding villages were all they knew, and yet they had no choice but to leave their world. Living in a rocky spot with too many folk scratching for too little food, poverty and hardship was their lot. Now they'd had their fill. Yet though the land had pushed them out, still the colly-wobbles of anxiety surged about their stomachs whilst stirrings of regret swirled about their minds.

An Italian Brummie making pure ices, 1920s. (Thanks to Mrs V. Iommi)

Like so many youngsters before and after, they trudged towards the coast, their sadness matched by a growing excitement about what lay ahead. At the rumbustious port of Naples they paid over most of their long-saved coins and boarded a ship for the west coast of England. The conditions on board were vile and by the time they reached Bristol they craved fresh air and light. After a few days in a dismal lodging house they set off once again.

Playing their accordions and mandolins in villages and market towns they busked their way eastwards, picking up a few coppers here and an odd bit of silver there. At last they reached their goal - the great working town of Birmingham. Traipsing along the tree-lined width of the Bristol Road they were astonished at the large houses with big front gardens which were cultivated for pleasure and not survival. They felt they'd come to a land of untold wealth, but as they crossed Sun Street and St Luke's Road everything changed. Here, the footpaths were heaving with people. It was loud, frantic and nerve-wracking. Mithered by the commotion, they were pushed into the horse road by the hustle of people.

Dodging the rumbling wheels of the wagons and the flicking whips of the carters, they reached the quietness of the doorway of St Catherine's in the Horsefair. Cheered up at finding a Catholic church, they went inside and sought a priest. Only speaking Nobladani - the Neapolitan dialect which was so different to Italian - they found it difficult to make themselves understood. Then one of them pulled from his pocket a scrap of paper. On it were scrawled the words '40 Bartholomew Street'. The priest nodded his head knowingly and took them on the last part of their travels.

Close to the Bull Ring and running off Digbeth, the street was cut in two by a railway line. It was narrow and dark, houses and small factories packed into as little an area as possible. Misty and overcast, the weather made the place seem even more sombre. What a difference to the clear

Each year in the 1930s Father Daley of St Michael's Church, Moor Street arranged for a trip by some of the lads in the boys' club to his brother's farm in Ireland. Carmen Tamburro is in the foreground of this photo. His family was renowned for its accordion playing and had a shop where they repaired accordions and gave lessons in their playing. The last one to run it was Jackie, who died in 1994.
(Thanks to Micky Volante)

Italian, Irish and English Brummies having a knees up at St Michael's Boys' Club, Moor Street, 1930s. Playing the piano is Norman Philips whose wife was one of the Frezzas. Seated are John McCoy, the teacher who got the sports teams off the ground at St Michael's and later became head; and Spud Murphy, who coached for Sir Matt Busby at Manchester United. Behind them at the back is Vincent Bastianelli, who owned a paper shop in Duddeston Row and who started the boys' club. The lady next to him is Mrs di Mascio, who ran a lodging house, and the other lady is Mrs Wellings. Just in view standing at the back and on the left is Tony Lanca; next to him and with the hat is Jackie Cunnington; and Joe Mattiello is the lad with the hair parted in the middle and the badge. In front of him is Joey Page; beneath the light is Norman Philips junior; and in front of him is Johnny Bacciochi. The youngsters standing to the left of the piano are (left to right) Mousey Sawyer, Pasquale Zacaroli, Sammy Fox and Peter Cunnington. Just in front of them and with the hat is Paul de Mascio who later served with the Royal Warwicks. On the other side, Alfie Volante – with the hand in front of his mouth – is in front of Mrs Wellings, whilst Philip Volante is leaning over the piano. Second from his left and with the hat on is Billy Higgins; on the left the lad with his face turned up is Johnny Forletter; and two from his right is Jackie Oliver. Above the piano with the pointed hat is Bobby Larkin and next to him is Joey Kennedy. (Thanks to Betty Mattiello, born Higgins, and to Joe Mattiello for the information)

skies and wide spaces of the Comino Valley! A feeling of homesickness welled up inside them, and yet as soon as they went inside the house, the distance from Italy seemed less. They knew everyone and they were greeted with Italian food. There was wine and macaroni, as well as flat beans and nyuks - flour and sausages rolled into a sausage shape. Those who'd come before them had made sure to fetch a bit of Italy to the middle of Brum.

Bartholomew Street and Duddeston Row were the hub of Birmingham's Italian Quarter. And what a contribution the families from Gallinaro and elsewhere have made to Brummagem! They brought us the best ice-cream in the world and they laid wonderful terrazzo floors in Dudley Road Hospital, the Odeon and so many more of our public buildings. The Italian Quarter of Old Brum was cleared in the redevelopment's of the 1950s. Many remember it with affection, not just for its feel but also for the way its people lived and collared together - Italian, English and Irish. Ciao!

WELSH WORKHORSES

Days and days ago they'd set off from their farm in Montgomeryshire. Fresh and fit, they'd gathered their cattle and headed off on the long journey eastwards. First they made for Welshpool, where they crossed the River Severn. Following its meandering path, they slowly and laboriously approached Shrewsbury. They'd stop there a night, giving themselves and their cattle a little time to rest up. Then they left the great river behind and as the hills of mid-Wales faded in the distance, they struck out across Shropshire. The rains had been heavy and they squelched tiredly along roads which were sodden and muddy, occasionally flicking the cows to keep them moving.

At last they spotted the spire of St Peter's and St Paul's, telling them Wolverhampton was near. Another short rest beckoned. Then it was on and into the parish of Birmingham. Ahead of them was

A class at Tiverton Road Girls' School, Bournbrook, 1930. Joan Harvard is seated at the front in the middle. Joan had a lovely, lilting South Welsh accent which is still etched in her daughter's memory. Sadly Joan died in 1943 when her daughter, Audrey, was just four. (Thanks to Audrey Broad)

The choir of Ada Road Secondary Modern School rehearsing for their carol service which was to be held at St Andrew's Church, Small Heath, 1949. The music master is Mr H. Osborne. Was he a Welshman? If not, there were many of us English schoolkids who were taught by Welsh teachers who tried to get us to sing tunefully!

their destination, the spot where they sold their cattle. It was at the junction of High Street, Dale End and Bull Street - and it was called the Welsh End.

Birmingham in the early 1500s was still a small place, but it was a growing one. Sheltering on the southern slopes of Bennet's Hill, it was gaining fame for its metal workers, it was attracting attention for its weavers and dyers, and it was demanding notice as a major market centre. It was this reputation as a trading place which drew in so many Welsh cattlemen - not only from Montgomeryshire but also from Radnorshire.

These Welsh folk were crucial in helping to feed the expanding number of Brummies, and where they gathered became a focal point in the town. In the early 1700s, an impressive cross was built there. It was a large square building with two open archways on each side. On Saturdays the floor space was used for the buying and selling of goods, whilst the upper half was a military guard-house. On the top of the structure was a small clock tower and a weather vane.

The Welsh Cross was knocked down in 1803 to allow for road widening, but the importance of the Welsh to Birmingham continued. In particular the Lloyd Family had a major impact. Coming from

Montgomeryshire in 1698, they set up Lloyd's Bank in 1765 on Dale End and helped to finance the expansion of Brum.

There were countless other Welsh immigrants to Birmingham, and until the middle of the nineteenth century it is likely that they were the most numerous group after the English. In a trades directory of 1818 there were listed 68 people with the name of Jones - second only in number to people called Smith. Their occupations were wide-ranging. They included teachers, bricklayers, butchers, blacksmiths, publicans, shopkeepers, jewellers, bakers, merchants and victuallers.

The Welsh were also crucial in the building of our Town Hall. This magnificent building is faced with marble, which was also used to make the Greek-style columns which adorn the hall's outside. The marble was given by Sir Richard Bulkley, who owned the Penmon Quarries in Anglesey, and it was fashioned by highly-skilled workers from that island.

The Welsh have never received the recognition they deserve for their part in making Birmingham. They've helped to feed us, they've taught us, they've financed our undertakings, and they've sung for us. They continue to sing for us with the world-famous Canoldir Choir.

Old Brum owes a great debt to the talents and hard work of Welsh Brummies. Perhaps it's time we had a Welsh Cross again.

The Welsh Presbyterian Church in Suffolk Street, 1957. This was registered for public worship in 1898 and replaced 'a small building at the foot of Bath Row' known as a Rehoboth Chapel and used from 1849. In turn this had succeeded a chapel in use from 1842 in Peck Lane. There was one other Welsh Presbyterian place of worship in Brum, at Hockley Hill.

KIND ERNIE, PRINCE OF BEGGARS:
ERNIE McCULLOCH

He'd had plenty of hard times himself, growing up in the back streets of Deritend and Digbeth. He'd known what it was like to be clammed and to have bosted old boots that wailed you. That's why he'd swore that when he got older he'd do whatever he could to mek life better for the poor kids of Brum.

His passion was bolstered by his deep religious beliefs. He was a regular at Carr's Lane Church, but he wasn't a once a week Christian. No, he went out every day doing what Jesus had done, preaching the Gospel, urging his fellows to love thy neighbour and holding out a hand of friendship and hope to the sick, the hurt, the skint and the unfortunate. No wonder they called Ernie McCulloch the Kindest Man in Brum.

Poverty and Christianity were the forces which made him. He fought against the one as he strove for the other. And what better battleground than Brum's Bull Ring? For more than 50 years he had made his way there each Sunday dinner-time and evening, drawing in listeners then coaxing and pressing

A day out for 'ragged children', about 1905. Kids like those were taken out to Sutton Park by Mr Pentland and later by his successor at the head of the Royal Robins, Ernie McCulloch. Amongst the ladies and gents at the back are the mom and dad of Fred Pickett both helpers on the trip. (Thanks to Joanna Pickett)

Ernie McCulloch surrounded with children in the Bull Ring, Sunday 11 February, 1959. The kids were clothed as a result of a collection from the crowd who gathered to hear Ernie a week previously.

them to give their coppers and silver for needy.

He'd first spoke in front of Nelson's Statue in 1903. Tall and slender and not yet 20, he knew he was called to do something for his own people. It wasn't an easy task. He had nothing to stand on and often he was lost in a bunch of onlookers. But soon he had his own pulpit. Ernie had done a good turn to an out-of-work chippie and when things picked up the carpenter made a platform in his attic. It was about three foot high, four foot square and had a little rail at the front. There was only one snag. It was too big to get down the stairs and so the chippie took out his window frame and with a clothes line he lowered the platform to the street!

Ernie med good use of that platform. It never took him long to pull an audience and he'd try anything to mek a few bob for a good cause. Once he even got a woman to tek off her gansey, flogging it eight times before he finally gave it her back! Another time, he raised over four quid by auctioning a penny packet of ten cigarettes.

Whatever the cause, you could guarantee that Ernie would be doing his bit. In the depression of the Thirties a column of hunger marchers stopped off in the Bull Ring on their long walk to London. They were fagged out and footsore and Ernie scrounged soap and towels for them so that they could wash their feet in the cloakrooms of Carr's Lane Church. Then he tore back down to St Martin's and begged bread and cheese from the good-hearted shoppers so that he could give the unemployed miners a meal!

There were so many things that Ernie was involved in. He was vice-chairman of the Hospital Saturday Fund, a visitor for convalescent cases in St Bartholomew's Ward, a representative of the Hay Mills and South Yardley Nursing Associations and a Divisional President of the St John Ambulance Brigade. That's as well as being life governor of the General Dispensary, the Children's Hospital, the General Hospital and The Birmingham and Midland Eye Hospital.

Even in his job he did good as Works Welfare Superintendent at Birmid in Smethwick. But above all it was kids who touched Ernie's heart. He'd regularly shout: "Ee are, pass us up that lad!" and when the youngster was with him on the platform he'd sell him for a dollar or more. That money was given to the Royal Robins, probably Ernie's favourite cause. Founded by Mr Pentland in 1893, each summer this charity took 3,000 odd kids to Sutton Park for a day out. And a thousand of the poorest were treated to a trip to the sea - something few of them had ever seen.

As they grew up the Robins never forgot him and on June 20th, 1948 they and hundreds of other Brummies packed into the Bull Ring to present him with an illuminated address and a travelling case.

True to his life's work, straight away Ernie used the bag to have a whip round for distressed children in Europe. When he died in 1964 it was reckoned that he'd raised over £100,000 for good causes and that he'd helped scores of thousands of Brummies. Ernie McCulloch: the Prince of Beggars of Old Brum.

Ernie McCulloch, 24 June 1964.

GRANDAD, WE LOVE YOU...

It was the best time of the week - the day his grandad minded him. Mostly when his mom was at work, he was looked after by an aunt. She was alright, but there was nobody could hold a light to his grandad. They were more like two pals, even though the one was little more than a babby whilst the other was greyed by the passing of time.

Every Friday, the routine was the same. The little lad would be up, swilled and dressed s'never his mom called him. He'd stand at the door fiddling with his hands and shifting his feet from side to side and when he was really fed up, he'd push his small donny into his mom's hand to tell her to get weaving. Off they'd set dead early 'cus she had to drop him off and then clock in. They were there soon enough because it was only a couple a three hundred yards away. Just an ordinary terraced house in a typical Brummagem street, but to the lad it was a wonderful world.

There was grandad waiting at the door, defying his years to swoop down and pick up his lad. Then the rituals and little games started. He'd pull the boy towards

Antonio and Antonia Tavolier outside their sweet shop in Duddeston Row, 1930s. Their granddaughter, Maria Sartori, is in the arms of Auntie Theresa, an Irish woman engaged to Maria's uncle. The family also had a fish and chip shop and sold ice cream. Antonia was a Bove by marriage and she and her husband were amongst the first Italians to settle long term in Birmingham – acting as a point of contact for relatives who migrated to the city later.
(Thanks to Maria Giansante and John Sartori)

My great grandad, William Wood, holding the hands of two of his grandsons, Our Johnny and Our Kenny Wood, about 1948/9. They're in the front garden of 7 back of 6, Whitehouse Street, the home of Our Nan and Grandad, Lil and Arthur Perry. The yard was bounded by the wall of St Mary's School and in the background are the brew'uses – wash-houses. Like many other blokes Our Grandad Perry used to try and brighten things up in the yard by growing sweet peas, carnations, geraniums and blue lobelia, whilst he used to make patterns in the garden with house bricks from the bomb peck. Most of Our Nan's family lived in the same street, including Great Granny and Grandad Wood, Uncle Bill, Uncle Bob, Aunt Win, Aunt Nance, Aunt May and their kids. (Thanks to Winnie Martin)

his unshaven face, ready to nuzzle him with whiskers that prickled - and the youngster would swing his head back, laughing out "Pack it up, Grandad!" His mom forgotten, she'd stride off leaving the old man to take over. "Alright, ma lad. Tell you what, how about some porridge, then I'll have me shave and we'll have a mooch down the paper shop and get you some cuckooks. Ow's that sound?" How did it sound? Bostin, of course.

They sat at the table in the back kitchen and canted to their hearts content as they scooped up the watery porridge. That's how grandad always made it, and it was smashing 'cus he reckoned grandad was always right. Then, the boy would sit with his knees pulled up to his chest and his chin cupped in his hands to watch the old man strop his open razor on a strap of leather, make up his lather and cut off the bristles.

"Now, ma lad, we're all shipshape and ready. Let's fetch the paper." Down the road they went and round the corner, his grandad doffing his panama at the older women he passed and swapping an "Alright" with a chap here and there. Into the shop they trooped for the *Sporting Buff*, a quarter of kayli and herbal drops.

Back home, they picked out the winners - they hoped - sucked rocks and dipped fingers into the rainbow sugar crystals. With three thr'penny double and a thr'penny cross treble written on the back of a Woodbine packet they were ready for the adventure of putting the bets on. Grandad had told him to watch out for the coppers and the lad turned his head hither and thither as they came towards the

bookie's runner. Full of collywobbles, he watched amazed as the old man leaned forward, muttered 'Gie us a light' and swiftly palmed away the bet as the tekker held out a match. The dangerous part over, they went for their reward. First off into the bread shop for a cottage loaf and a couple of dripping cakes, then to the cooked meat shop for a quarter of ox-tongue, and last into the outdoor for a jug of mild ale.

Back in the house, grandad fetched a couple of the juicy tomatoes he grew in the back garden and a feast beckoned. As they chomped their way through their dinner, he poured a glass of ale and, through the side of his eye, watched the lad. He knew what the youngster wanted and although it was too hot really, he'd lit the fire specially for this part of the day. Over to the flames he went, picked up the poker and thrust it into the flames. As soon as it reddened, he took it out and dipped it into his glass of beer. The boy's eyes beamed as the ale raged and sizzled around the hot metal. That was the signal. He jumped on his grandad's lap and before the foam had dowted, he was given a sip of mild.

They always had a kip after dinner and when they woke up, grandad would tell him tales of life in the trenches and then send him to Burden's on the Lane to fetch the best ice cream in the world. "Mind the horse road, and don't tell y'r mother I've let y'goo on y'r own," he'd warn. I never did, grandad.

Me aged about 18 months with Our Grandad Chinn in 1958. Our Grandad always wore a panama in the summer, as he's doing here on our trip to Tommy Monk's pub at Earlswood. Our Jeffery, Our Uncle Bernard's son, is with me on the see-saw and I'm held by Our Uncle Ron. Sadly Ronnie died a few months after this photo was taken. He was just 31.

HEARTS OF GOLD:
EVENING MAIL CHRISTMAS TREE FUND

Birmingham in the 1800s - it was the workshop of the world. Old Brum was a place whose people were renowned for their craft and their skills. Deftly and artistically, they made a multitude of wares from steel pen nibs to steam engines, from coins to bicycles, from jewellery to brass bedsteads, from stained glass windows to guns. Birmingham was brash, bold and bursting with confidence. It was a place on the march, constantly moving forward, incessantly looking to the future. It was a great working town - adventurous, keen and prosperous.

But in the midst of plenty there was much hardship and deprivation. Great numbers of Brummies were low paid or casually employed. Poverty stalked their lives, whether or not they were skilled or unskilled, English or Irish, Italians or Jews, women or men, children or adults. Their lives were dominated by an uncertain income, by visits to the pawnshop and by life in badly-built and insanitary back-to-backs. The symbols of poverty were everywhere - from the stench that rose out of overflowing suffs and miskins to the tumbledown houses and unmade roads. You could see the poverty from the washing of the women in dilapidated brew'uses to the hawking of goods by bare-foot kids.

Boys from Jenkins Street School, Small Heath, 1918. Frank Culm is standing in the centre wearing the gansey and recalls that most of the lads wore boots given by the Birmingham Daily Mail Christmas Tree Fund. (Thanks to Frank Culm)

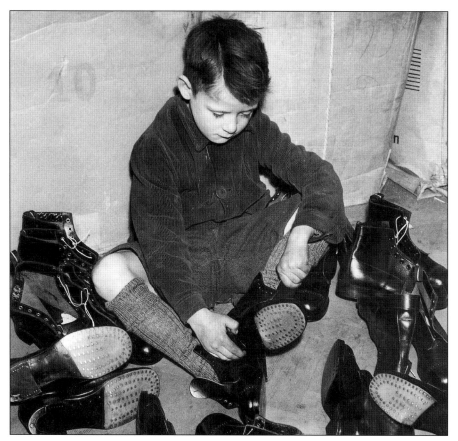

The distribution of Daily Mail boots in 1936 – look at those hob nails.

But throughout the century some good-hearted citizens tried to help the hungry, the unlucky and the unfortunate. Amongst them were journalists on the Birmingham *Daily Mail* and in 1889 the newspaper's owners acted decisively. They set up a 'Christmas Tree Fund' to raise money for 'toys and cash to brighten the lives of poor children in hospital'.

The idea caught the imagination of Brummies - and not just of the better-off, either. Reports of the day show that contributions poured in "from obscure back streets", delivered "secure in all sorts of recepticles from old cigar boxes and tin cans to ginger beer bottles and public swear boxes."

Soon the income raised from numerous small donations was so large that it was possible to extend the scope of the Fund. In 1906, it was decided that poor children would be given a Christmas dinner in Smithfield Market - although in subsequent years the food was given out in Bingley Hall so that families could take it home to cook themselves, often using coal also received free from the *Mail*. For the dinner in Smithfield, no less than 67 large tables were laid out and around 3,000 children tucked in to a festive feast.

During the same year the Fund started to give out specially-made boots to kids who walked about without shoes. It is a sobering thought to realise that this was happening in the wealthiest nation in the world, but neither the state nor local authorities acted to stop this scandal. Bare-foot children disappeared from the streets of Birmingham solely because of the determination of the *Mail* and the enthusiastic support of tens of thousands of ordinary Brummies who gave what money they could to the Christmas Tree Fund.

The significance of their actions was emphasised by the city's Chief Educational Officer. He declared that "in inclement weather it is absolutely cruel to require a child to go to school if it is insufficiently

clothed or has not got good boots. The Fund, in the character of the work it carries on, is absolutely unique."

Where the *Mail* led, other British and Irish newspapers followed, and similar charities were set up in Dublin, Manchester, Glasgow and elsewhere. In 1925 the Fund received royal praise - from Her Majesty Queen Alexandra. "The Queen is delighted to hear of the success of your fund," a telegraph message from the Palace went, "She wishes all the poor children and families who benefit by it a blessed and happy Christmas." When the message was read out aloud in Smithfield Market, some 7,000 children - all wearing their *Mail* boots - let out a mighty cheer.

Prime Minister Joseph Chamberlain added his support, too. "Best good wishes for your Christmas parties, with high appreciation of the labours which have brought about so successful a result," he wrote.

Bare-foot children may have disappeared from the streets of Birmingham, but there are many people who are still in need. And, as in 1889, they can look for assistance to the Christmas Tree Fund. It now operates a fleet of community mini-buses, carrying the elderly, handicapped and infirm around the region.

Just as much as in the past the Birmingham Mail Christmas Tree Fund continues to be of significance. Its success is due to one crucial thing - a remarkable partnership between generous Brummies and our own campaigning paper, the *Evening Mail.*

Eight-year-old Hubert Murray from Vauxhall and a pupil at Dartmouth Street School choosing his Daily Mail boots, late 1930s.

DOWN THE
OLD END

STREETS AHEAD:
ASTON HIGH STREET

Most towns have one High Street, but Brum's got eight – telling of the time when some of our districts were separate places, each with its own major shopping street. There's High Street, Birmingham, of course, and High Streets in Deritend, Bordesley, Harborne, Kings Heath, Saltley and Quinton. And there's also High Street, Aston.

This main street really was high. Starting at Six Ways, it swept down Potter's Hill to Phillips Street and the Hockley Brook – the southern boundary of Aston until the town was swallowed up by Brum in 1911. But the loss of independence didn't lead to a decline of the local High Street. It stayed the focal point for all the folk who lived in the little streets which ran off it, and more than that it drew people from nearby Lozells, Birchfield and Summer Lane.

No wonder they came here in their droves because High Street, Aston, had everything a shopper could wish for. It was packed with well-known retailers. There was Elizabeth Black's, the draper's which

opened for business as far back as 1885 and which sold ladies and children's wear. It lay behind four plate-glass windows and had a distinctive square glass showcase around which you could walk.

And who can forget the unusually-named "The House that Jack Built"? Taking up five premises, this department store was owned by Lewis S. Richards Ltd and if it was

A cold and wet afternoon hasn't stopped the folk of Alma Street, Aston setting up the tables and celebrating the coronation of our Queen on 2 June 1953. Alma Street was the birthplace of Albert Ketelby, one of the greatest English composers of light classical music and famed for compositions such as 'In a Monastery Garden'.

A cracking and unusual view of High Street, Aston at the time of a culverting of the Hockley Brook, 6 August 1953. The Aston Hippodrome is in the background and you can just make out Foster's at 158, High Street – between Burlington Street and Webster Street. Nearer at hand on the right is a branch of Harley's the shoe repairers, then a Baines's bread shop on the corner of Philips Street followed by the 'Dog and Duck' pub. On the other side of the road, close to the junction with Asylum Road can be seen the Co-op and Gould's the tailor's on the corner of Inkerman Street.

household goods you wanted, you got them here. It was overflowing with furniture and floor coverings, cutlery and crockery, sheets and pillows, pots and pans, and so much more besides. Our Nan said that in the 1920s when our Granny Wood, was pregnant, she'd go there to buy terryline at 6d a yard and flanelette at 3d a yard to make her own nappies and baby blankets, embroidering them with herringbone stitch. With winsiette she also made beds for the wenches – underskirts with a split up the front and tied around the waist.

There were shops of every kind along the High Street. If it was cheaper kitchenware you were after, the Penny Bazaar was for you, whilst if you needed shoes then the staff at Timpson's were happy to oblige. Women could get their millinery from Roberts's, and blokes could buy their clothes from Gould's, Hawkin's and Foster Brothers. Then there was Kate Vokes, the tobacconist, William Izon the chemist, the pawnshops of Pawson's and Biddles's, and the corn dealer's of Simpson's.

Most of all, what a feast of food outlets tempted your taste buds! High Street had grocers like Mason's, the Home and Colonial and Pearke's Dairies; there were high-class confectioners such as Greasley-Norton's, bread shops like Wimbush's and Baines's – and a specialist tea-seller called Edgerton. It hosted a coffee house owned by the famed Jelfs, a dining room run by those noted Italian Brummies the Iommis, and a celebrated greengrocer's called Griffin's selling fruit and fish, poultry and rabbits – each one skinned and chopped for just 9d.

And what about all those butchers? Do you recall Darrall's, Harry Smith's, Norris's and Walter Smith's as well as Samuel Procter, who was known for auctioning his meat on a Saturday night, and Mr Smart who was praised for his kindness in giving cag mag to the poor. Bywaters were talked about for their pork, and W Richards was renowned for his succulent sausages, hams, bacon, lard and scratchings.

But High Street wasn't just about shopping, it was also a centre of entertainment. Just off the main drag in Potter's Lane stood the Aston Hippodrome across whose boards walked Laurel and Hardy, Gracie Fields, George Formby and Brummagem's own Sid Field. If they fancied it, the performers could have a swift half in the magnificent 'Barton's Arms' with its stunning tiles and snob screens which gave privacy to a shy drinker.

Smaller, more intimate pubs included the 'Dog and Duck' and the 'Scotch House' – but these weren't the only centres of leisure. There was Burlington Hall with its clubs and branch of the St John's Ambulance Brigade and there were two picture houses – the eastern-style Orient and the Globe with its striking dome and wooden benches.

No need to go up town when in High Street you could buy whatever you wanted, have fun or just have a mooch. What a pity the council ignored its vitality and allowed a dual carriageway to thunder through and destroy its buildings. That was High Street, Aston – made by its people and ruined by redevelopment.

Another view of Aston High Street, clearly showing the 'Dog and Duck' and the celebrated store 'The House That Jack Built', 1960s. The end of the High Street as a thriving shopping centre is heralded by the corrugated iron shutting up Bywater's the noted pork butcher's. (Thanks to Johnny Landon)

BUILDING A COMMUNITY:
BALSALL HEATH

Balsall Heath at the dawning of the 1800s. On its western boundary, the River Rea flows clean and fresh, filled with small fish and even pike. Rising from the water is lush, partly wooded land. Along the ridge above the river runs the turnpike road to Alcester, later the Moseley Road, with old-fashioned toll gates at Kyrwicks Lane. And eastwards to the Spark Brook is a flat expanse of countryside, the heath which gave its name to the whole district.

The views from the high ground of the Moseley Road are stunning. Northwards is the land-hungry Birmingham with the steeple of St Martin's pointing proudly upwards, and St Philip's Cathedral dominating Bennetts Hill. Westwards is the picturesque Edgbaston Church surrounded by parkland, and

Balsall Heath Swimming and Washing Baths, just before the First World War. Built in 1906 with red brick and terracotta in the impressive Gothic Renaissance style, it boasts a Free Library next door. Both facilities were constructed as part of the deal to encourage Balsall Heath Local Board of Health ratepayers to vote to abandon their independence and join Birmingham – which they did in 1891. The swimming baths have two pools, the larger of which is overlooked by a spectators' gallery. The washing baths are still in use. (Thanks to Mike Tunnicliffe)

Peter and John (the bigger lad) Hemming outside the huckster's shop of their mom and dad, Walter and Lucy Hemming, at 221, Balsall Heath Road, about 1936. What a cracking window filled with everything the local folk needed! The shop was almost opposite Mary Street and sold mainly sweets, chocolates and cigarettes. Other goods included bread, butter, sugar, milk, vinegar, firewood, washing soap and home-made ice cream on Saturdays and Sundays in the summer. Strangely the Hemmings stocked good, cheap watches – some of which can be seen on the right-hand side of the window display. This was because Walter knew a man in the trade who lived next door to his sister in Belgrave Road. (Thanks to Peter Hemming)

to the south west can just be made out the Bromsgrove Lickey Hills. The only industry is the tannery of Henry Homer, near to which the 'Castle and Falcon' pub would stand later.

No wonder this location appealed to prosperous middle class men like Thomas Haden, whose family made its wealth from button making. His home, beautifully situated on Highgate Hill, was a substantially built dwelling – "the staircase being of stone and the entrance hall was flagged, beneath which were excellent cellars". The property also boasted gardens, plantations, a lawn, and a highly productive old pasture ground.

When Haden died in 1837, his land was sold for building and Belgrave Road was cut through it. The adjoining farms were transformed in the same way. Sherborne and Balsall Heath Roads were developed on the Frowd Estate, whilst the property of the Reverend Vincent Edwards was pierced by streets named after him and his wife Mary.

Despite the opening of the railway line to Gloucester in 1840, the area between the Moseley Road and Ladypool Lane stayed rural. Apart from the emergence of Clifton and Brighton Roads there was little building until 1853, when the Birmingham Freehold Land Society developed the Balsall Heath Estate around White Street.

By this time the whole district was described as 'a new town' and its population had risen rapidly from a few score to several thousands. It had a Methodist Chapel in Vincent Street, the Anglican St Paul's and the Catholic St John the Evangelist churches, regular horse-drawn bus services to Birmingham city centre and a private open-air swimming bath in George Street.

Yet the district still belonged to Kings Norton – a huge, agricultural parish which was unable to cope with the needs of urban Balsall Heath. Unsurprisingly, its people demanded independence and in 1862 their aim was achieved. The Balsall Heath Local Board of Health was formed with powers to repair and improve the local streets and to make other sanitary improvements. Based at offices in Lime Grove, it did a good job but in 1891 the lure of Brum proved too great and the ratepayers voted to join their bigger neighbour.

By now the district's last rural remnants had gone. Longmoore Farm by the Rea was sold in 1869; Ladypool Farm by St Paul's Road was built on soon after; and the Watkins Estate was cut through with Ombersley Road in the late 1880s. During the same period houses marched between Stoney Lane and the Ladypool Road, sweeping away "the quaint old farmhouse" of Sam Melson, his fertile fields and the training ground for his small stud of race-horses.

Balsall Heath had become a crucial part of Birmingham. It had a population of over 30,000 and a number of important businesses – such as builder John Bowen of George Street, responsible for the construction of the Law Courts in Corporation Street, and the Mozart Works of Sames Pianos in Woodfield Road. These are sadly no more, but there remain well-established firms like Camera Bellows in St Paul's Road and Ryland's Paints in Haden Street; as well as Butcher's Printed Products and Alfred Parker's Gun Makers on the Moseley Road.

This thoroughfare is almost like a civic centre in the grandeur of some of its buildings. Just look at them: the Congregational and Methodist Chapels; the imposing Moseley and Balsall Heath Institute; an old tram depot; the former Moseley Road Art School; the one-time 'Imperial' Picture House, and the magnificent red-brick library and public swimming baths.

Balsall Heath has a proud past. Its people are determined its future will be as impressive.

Minni Faulkener outside her home in Main Terrace, Wenman Street, June 1962. Within a few years this terrace and many others were to be swept away by redevelopment. Wenman Street itself used to run from Balsall Heath Road to Edward Road, but now it's been cut in half.

SHRUNKEN MANOR:

BORDESLEY

How the mighty have shrunk! Today, if you search for Bordesley, then signposts would indicate that it's a small spot on the western slope of Kingston Hill, stretching down from the Blues ground to the heaving Middle Ring Road which almost obliterates what used to be Watery Lane. True, just past there can be found Bordesley Station, its entrance almost hidden below the railway bridge at the bottom of the Cov. And that road itself flows into Bordesley High Street which still runs from Camp Hill to its junction with High Street, Deritend.

These names only hint at the once wider and broader Bordesley of the Middle Ages when it was a manor in its own right. Taking its name from the Anglo-Saxon 'Borda's Ley' - the clearing of Borda - it extended over almost 1900 acres and reached close to the Bull Ring. Bordesley was actually cut off from Brum by the River Rea, while it was divided from Yardley to the south and south east by the Spark Brook and River Cole. To the south west the boundary with Kings Norton was also sharp, provided as it was by the Highgate Road and Belgrave Road; but to the north east the demarcation with Saltley and Little

A poster for the 'Bordesley Palace', 1903. Formerly the 'Imperial', the building had been purchased recently by Moss Empires for £6,000.

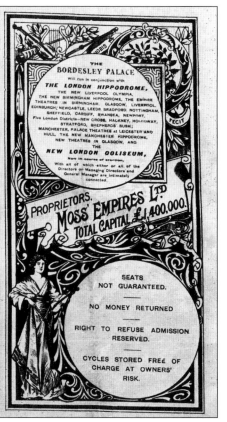

Shaw's shop on the corner of Adderley Street and New Bond Street, 1950s. The house next door was that of Joyce Biddle's Auntie Gert. She had a front room which was always perfect. Next door to her was the home of Joyce's Granny Gray. In the background, beyond the lorries is the 'Barrel' pub where Granny Gray used to get her jug of beer. Previously Shaw's shop had been owned by Mr and Mrs Bonas who lived there with their six girls and three boys. The eldest son, Thomas, was a well-known street trader in fruit and veg in Greenway Street, Small Heath. Mrs E. Hanson recalls helping her dad pushing a three-wheeler basket carriage from the wholesale fruit and veg market in the Bull Ring back home at about 6.30 in the morning. The basket carriages were hired for 4½d from a place in Heath Mill Lane where two men used to sit all day weaving and completing them. Mr Bonas also kept a horse at the back of the house in New Bond Street, using it to take the family out in a trap on Sunday evenings in the summer. (Information thanks to Joycie Biddle, born Gray; Mrs Jean Bonas; and Mrs E. Hanson)

Bromwich was less clear, hugging as it did the skirts of Garrison Lane. So Bordesley actually spread out from the 'Triangle' at Gooch Street to the 'Era' on the corner of Churchill Road, from the BSA in Armoury Road to Bird's Custard in Gibb Street, and from Itchy Coo Rec to Farm Park.

In the time of Elizabeth 1, the manor was held by the Ardens and when the male line of the family died out it was split among four sisters. One of them was married to Sir Charles Adderley of Lea, whose name is recalled in a modern street. His son later sold his land in Bordesley and by the 1700s much of the district was owned by the Holtes, who also possessed Aston, Duddeston and Nechells. Unlike Deritend which developed as an extension of Birmingham from our earliest beginnings as a market town, the rest of Bordesley stayed rural for centuries. Large tracts of farmland were leased out by great landowners like the Digbys and Goochs and the area even boasted its own imposing hall. Constructed on Mount Pleasant in 1750, it was owned by John Taylor - the Brummagem button king who joined forces with Sampson Lloyd to start the bank which now carries the name of the Welsh family alone.

Cut through as it was by the major routes from Coventry and Stratford which merged at the bottom of Camp Hill, Bordesley was ripe for development. By the 1820s buildings had filled in the length of its high street, while to the west the land had been urbanised between Birchall Street, Moseley Street and Stratford Place.

On the east change was less obvious. Adderley Street and Upper Trinity Street were present but much of the land was in use as small gardens, although these soon disappeared as Glover Street, Palmer Street and Great Barr Street burst into history. Increasingly threatened by the outpouring of Birmingham, Bordesley lost its independence in 1838. The take-over by its bigger neighbour was followed rapidly by the sale of Taylor's Bordesley Hall estate and the emergence of Bordesley Park Road and Arthur Street. More and more fresh streets rapidly transformed the look of the district, and as they did so parts of the old manor began to be called differently.

Deritend was formally detached in 1873 when it became a ward in its own right, taking with it Bordesley High Street; and Highgate and Camp Hill both became recognised as distinct neighbourhoods. Nearby, Sparkbrook quickly made its presence felt either side of the Stratford Road, while Bordesley Green came into view more gradually. The most spectacular emergence of all was that of Small Heath. Formerly just the locality by Green Lane, it confidently marched outwards - perhaps helped in 1875 by the formation of Small Heath Alliance Football Club and its quick move to a ground in Muntz Street.

Despite the erection of the Bordesley Palace music hall in 1899, Bordesley was doomed to diminish. In 1911 the council abolished it as a distinct ward, splitting it between Small Heath and Sparkbrook. Yet Bordesley did not vanish altogether. The Brummies of its High Street and its hinterland held on fast to the ancient name and recently it's made a comeback. For one of the successes of the Heartlands Corporation must be referring to the development around St Andrew's Road as Bordesley Village.

Arthur Crowton standing with his mother and his wife outside Causer's coffee house in Watery Lane, 1950s. Jennifer Causer, a grandaughter, remembers well the sound of the crowds going to the Blues on a Saturday afternoon and still can taste the smoked haddock and poached egg with a piece that her grandmother would serve for their tea. On the corner of St Andrew's Road is Amison's the butcher's, which was run by Harry A. Senior and his son Harry W. (Information thanks to Arthur Crowton, Jennifer Causer and Irene Amison)

WORTH MORE THAN BRUM:
ERDINGTON

The crime appalled the people of Brum. Mary Ashford, 'a pretty country girl' from Erdington, went to a hop at the 'Tyburn House' pub on May 26th, 1817. The next morning she was found drowned in a marl pit in Penns Lane. Abraham Thornton, a bricklayer from Castle Bromwich, had danced with Mary for much of the night and was accused of her murder. He was acquitted, but the local folk were unconvinced of his innocence and Mary's younger brother brought a private prosecution against Thornton.

The November trial was startling. When asked how he pleaded the defendant declared: "not guilty; and I am ready to defend the same with my body." He then delved into his counsel's bag and grasped a pair of leather gloves. Putting one on his left hand, he threw the other gauntlet at the feet of William Ashford, so challenging him to a duel.

Everyone in the courtroom was electrified. Such a response had not been heard since 1638. Faced with a burlier and stronger opponent, William withdrew his charge. Soon after, wager by battle was abolished and Thornton emigrated to America – unable to dispel the suspicions against him. Strangely,

Workers at Nock's Brickwords, Erdington, 1890.

High Street Erdington in the 1920s. Mable Coulborn's china shop is on the left at No. 120 and next door with the canopy down is Roland Benton's paper shop. In the background is St Barnabas's Church.

more than 500 years before this case the lord of the manor was a Giles de Erdington and faced with a dispute over the boundaries of his lands he had also challenged his opponent to a duel and won.

His family had gained their property following the Norman conquest of England. According to the Domesday Book, in 1086 the manor of Erdington had arable land for six ploughs, a mill rated at three shillings a year, five acres of meadows and a wood. It was worth 30 shillings – ten bob more than Birmingham! The name itself probably means the farm (ton) of Earda's people (ing), although the place has also been known as Hardintone and Yenton – that's why Erdingtonians can also be Yentonians.

Until the middle of the 19th century no more than a couple of thousand people ever lived in Erdington, yet some of them played a crucial part in the development of Birmingham. There was John Jennens, a wealthy ironmonger who sold to the nation the goods made by the smiths of Brum. In the 1650s he had a forge at Bromford Mill and lived at Erdington Hall, on the site of the old manor house by the River Tame – close to the junction of Wheelwright Road and Tyburn Road. Then there was Josiah Mason, the pen king of Brum. Once he'd made his money with Perry's Pens in the 1840s, he moved out to Norwood House – between Silver Birch Road and Holly Lane and now the site of Sir Edward Campion School. He's recalled by a road name and a bust on the Chester Road. It's close to Orphanage Road, which remembers the home for orphans which he set up nearby.

Mason died in Erdington in 1881, and although Gravelly Hill was now lined with large houses for wealthy Brummies most of the district was still farmland, and fishermen caught trout in the Tame. The village itself was "a straggling hamlet given to agricultural pursuits, with a shop here and there grouped round about the parish church".

But as the 19th century waned Erdington was set for spectacular change. Its population swept past 10,000 and in 1894 it broke away from Aston and became an Urban District Council. The councillors were a cute bunch of blokes. Not wishing to spend money on their own services they bought gas and water from Birmingham, while they struck deals with Aston for electricity, fire-brigade services and treatment for hospital cases. They even got the millionaire Andrew Carnegie to pay for the building of a library at a cost of £6,000!

Brum finally swallowed up Erdington in 1911 and five years later Dunlop moved its production of tyres from Aston to a new factory in Erdington – with many of its employees brought to work up the cut on specially-adapted narrow boats. Later Fisher and Ludlow's also set up in the same locality, joining well-established firms like Nock's the brickmakers.

Erdington has continued to be of importance industrially with major firms like SP Tyres and it's also had an effect on the entertainment world. What about the celebrated Mother's Nightclub on the High Street? And, of course, there's the connection with the film star Anne Heywood - once an usherette called Violet Pretty at Erdington's 'Palace Picture House'. With the new Jaguar plant, Erdington is certain to keep on making its mark – as it has done throughout its history.

The winner of the **Sunday Mercury** *walk passing Erdington Abbey, about 1937 or 1938*.

GREEN THAT VANISHED:
GOSTA GREEN

A smashing view of Gosta Green with the library behind the tree in the foreground, 1920s.

We've all got a powerful image of what a Green should be like. In our mind's eye it's a peaceful and idyllic scene from Olde England, a grass-covered plot which is the focal point of a rural village. It's hemmed in by a church and black and white timbered buildings, and around its edges old men sit smoking their clay pipes whilst they watch younger blokes bowling or playing cricket.

Even in the midst of huge, noisy and boisterous Brum there are two spots which can evoke such dreams of Merrie England. They're The Green at Kings Norton and The Green at Castle Bromwich. Quiet and peaceful, they bring to life the rural past of Birmingham. Once there were plenty of other greens locally, but they've disappeared under the relentless onslaught of a city hungry for land to use for housing, factories, transport and public buildings.

Yet if the greens of Old Brum are no more, at least they're recalled in the names of many districts. There's Winson Green, Acocks Green, Stockland Green, Bordesley Green, Hall Green, Yardley Green, Wake Green and Nechells Green. And, of course, there's Gosta Green.

Today Gosta Green is hidden behind the bulk of the Central Fire Station and is overshadowed by the towering structures of Aston University. Few Brummies now live around here and sadly the name has disappeared from maps of modern Brum. It shouldn't have - because it has a long history. It's called after William de Gorsty, who lived in the locality as far back as 1306, and for centuries it was right on the outskirts of Birmingham.

It included the area between Stafford Street (now James Watt Queensway) in the west, Aston Street in the north, Coleshill Street in the south and Duke Street in the east - which was the border with Aston.

As Brum expanded outwards, this agricultural land was cut into streets. There was Vauxhall Street, pointing towards the pleasure gardens of that name in Duddeston, and Butts Lane and Cross Street. These two places recalled the days in the Middle Ages when the men of Birmingham practiced their archery locally by shooting arrows at Butts Cross. Old Cross Street is still there, but Butts Lane is now Ryder Street, although for a while it was also known as Tanter Street.

By the early twentieth century this small part of Birmingham was packed with back-to-backs, it was crowded with Brummies who knew how to collar and to graft, and it was filled with significant buildings. In Lawrence and Ryder Streets stood the first council houses built in Brum. Nearby in Gem Street there was a school of deaf children as well as Bishop Ryder's Church - remembering the bishop of Lichfield whose efforts led to its erection in 1838.

Some of the girls of Bishop Ryder's School in Gem Street, Gosta Green, about 1922. Elsie Studley remembers that the teachers were very strict but very fair. Most of the kids were poor but there were some 'posh ones' who were the children of publicans and caretakers at the County Courts. They wore beautiful dresses and real kids shoes on the Anniversary Day at the church.
(Thanks to Elsie Studley, born Rowley)

A close up of the 'Old Peacock' pub, 1930s. It was closed down before the Second World War ready to be demolished for the proposed Aston University. Its last gaffer was Mr Newey and his son took this snap.
(Thanks to Irene Newey)

Then on the corner of Coleshill Street and Gem Street there was the 'Gaiety' Picture House, on the site of Brum's first music hall - 'Holder's'. Almost next door in Sheep Street there rose up Kyrle Hall, a renowned centre for sport and education, whilst in Duke Street there was one of the city's oldest police stations which dated back to 1847. Nearby were the swimming and washing baths at Woodcock Street, opened in 1860. Many of us have vivid and fond memories of the school swimming competitions which were always held at these magnificent baths.

But the throbbing heart of the whole thriving neighbourhood was Gosta Green itself, bestriding the junctions of Aston Road, Legge Street, Fisher Street, Aston Street, Duke Street, Woodcock Street and Lister Street. A cobble-stone open space - that's all it looked - but it was more than that as thousands of Brummies realised.

Although they were only small and unassuming, a horse trough and a drinking fountain dominated Gosta Green. Generations of kids grew up believing that in the top of the fountain there lived a monkey which would jump out at you if you dared to climb on his building! A good tale and one which kept youngsters out of mischief.

On the Lister Street side of the Green there was the 'Delicia' Picture House, which was well-known for holding wrestling competitions. Across the way, and on the triangle which joined Legge Street and Aston Road, there was a library, which began lending books in 1868. And on the Green, women wardrobe dealers gathered, laying out their second-hand clobber on the floor and trying to knock it for as much as they could.

The map makers ought to restore Gosta Green. Its name, its people, its buildings-all were crucial in the making of Brum.

WORKING DAY AND NIGHT:
HARBORNE

Hard collar was the only thing they knew. Each day they rose before dawn, swilling their faces with cold water, trying to fling the sleep from their minds as much as from their bodies. In the spring and summer they headed off to the fields, labouring for the local farmers - digging, shifting, tilling, scything, fetching, carrying and doing whatever else they could so as to earn a few bob and stay free of the workhouse.

Once the harvest was in, they were laid off and, with no money coming in, they had to scrat to make do. They held fast to their little homes, rarely going into the street. In the dark and cold days of winter they left their small cottages mostly to toil in small workshops in their yards.

Staff at the Harborne Post Office, early 1900s. (Thanks to Betty Hunt)

Pamela Smith is the buttercup lady at the back in this photo of a street party in Gray's Road, Harborne to celebrate the Coronation of our Queen on 2 June 1953. Pamela's brother is the scarecrow in the front and won first prize in the fancy dress competition. Malcolm Joes is the chef, the clown was a lad called Morris and the little girl was named Linda. (Thanks to Pamela Smith)

Noises rang out from the working-class terraces of Harborne - and rarely was there a silent hour. From early morning until deep into the night hammers clinked, bellows wheezed, anvils clanged, forges spat, and metal sang in a sad and melancholic way. Whole families grafted together and even mothers with babies joined in. They strapped their infants on to their backs, snuggling them into cloth bags, so that they could mind them and still labour.

The children swiftly became adults, learning the craft of hand-made nailing from when they were seven and eight years old. The routine was the same, whatever the age. The bellows were squeezed to excite the fire and with skill and dexterity the nailer thrust an iron rod into the rising flames.

When the metal was white hot, it was pulled out and with a small hammer one end of the rod was pounded and shaped until it had a head of the required width and thickness. That done, the nail was shoved back into the blaze before it was doused in water and dropped onto a pile in the corner.

Each Saturday morning the old man would leave his family at work and gathering the week's nails in an urden sack he would trudge into Brum. Here he'd flog his wares to a master who would sell them on to be hammered into tea chests. With his meagre earnings the nailer brought more rods for fashioning, so that he'd be lucky to be left with thirteen bob.

These were the wages of starvation - and the folk survived only because they grew things and had some hens and a pig. No wonder that the hand-made nailers declined in number and had all but disappeared by the 1880s. Faced with competition from factories which mass produced nails, they

abandoned their forges, left their homes and moved into Birmingham, looking for better-paid work in the great works of the city.

Their flight was matched by the transformation of Harborne itself. The village was centred on the 'King's Arms' in High Street, close to the junction with Harborne Park Road - although there were also hamlets at Harborne Heath by Nursery Road, and at the 'Kings Head' on the Hagley Road.

The whole area was in Staffordshire and as late as the early 1840s it had less that 2,000 people - but amongst them were two important residents. There was Thomas Attwood, the Birmingham banker who led the campaign to get the vote extended to the middle class, who lived at Grove Park. And there was David Cox, the son of a Brummie whitesmith and probably England's greatest artist after Constable and Turner, who had his home in Greenfield Road.

By the mid-1800s new streets were appearing, Harborne's population was expanding and it had a Local Board of Health. This body was elected by the ratepayers and was responsible for drainage, sewerage, street lighting and the removal of nuisances. But just like Balsall Heath, Ward End and Saltley, Harborne's independence was lost in 1891 when it was swallowed up by Brum. As part of the deal the local police force was increased from six to nine men and a free library was built.

By the 1920s Harborne High Street was a hive of activity, stretching from Nursery Road and Metchley Lane in the east and to Lordswood Road and Albert Road in the west. It had two picture houses, the 'Royalty' and the 'Harborne', a Baptist Chapel, St John's War Memorial Hall, a Young Men's Bible Association, a Salvation Army Citadel, social clubs, a dispensary for animals, pubs, a post office, schools, a police station and a variety of shops. Harborne High Street remains a thriving shopping centre - but it still has the feel of the village and traces linger of those hard-grafting but ill-paid folk who made nails which went around the world.

Alfred and Florence Brown outside their greengrocery shop in Vivian Road, Harborne, 12 April 1981. The business was started a century before by Florence's grandad, George Douce. He was followed by his second oldest son, Arthur – Florence's dad.

POWER OF THE MILL:

HAY MILLS

Imagine an age where there's no gas or electricity to make a big machine turn. Apart from a person's hands, the only source of power is water. That's why mills are everywhere in Old Brum, harnessing the flow of water and making huge stones move. But they aren't only for grinding corn. There are paper mills, rolling mills and slitting mills, as well as blade mills which grind edge tools, cutlery and swords.

After the coming of steam most of these mills disappeared, but many of their names are remembered in modern Birmingham. Over in Nechells by the Hockley Brook there's Thimblemill Lane, whilst in Hall Green near the River Cole there's Sarehole Mill. And on the River Rea there's both Heath Mill Lane and Duddeston Mill Road, whilst in Edgbaston by the Bourn Brook there's the BBC Studios at Pebble Mill.

But there's only one district of Brum which is named after a mill - and that's Hay Mills. It's a small spot, not far from the great island at the junction of the Small Heath Bypass and the Coventry Road. Yet if you ignore the roar of the frantic traffic and take a look down The Fordrough then it's an almost rural setting. Behind the foliage of a line of trees babbles the River Cole, and you can imagine the kingfishers

Tay's well-known butcher's shop on the Coventry Road, Hay Mills, 1911. At this time Hay Mill was a village in Worcestershire – separated from Brum by the River Cole and then the fields of Hay Barn and Little Hay farms in Small Heath. Tays continued trading as the neighbourhood changed into a thriving working-class suburb with a bustling shopping centre. The family carried on serving Hay Mills folk despite the ill effects of a 1980s road-widening scheme on the local shopkeepers.

Norman and Irene Benson outside their radio and television shop at the bottom of Kings Road at the junction with the Coventry Road, 17 April 1978. Like Tays, the Bensons were long-established in Hay Mills. The business was started in 1921 by Norman's dad, Harold. His wife was born on the premises when it was her father's building yard – whilst her grandfather was one of the founders of the local Congregational Church. After opening with crystal sets, Harold Benson used the back of the premises for a small electronics factory and turned one of the other buildings into a sweet shop. All the businesses were blighted and then ended by the Coventry Road Expressway in the 1980s.

singing as once they did. On the opposite bank can just be spied the tower of a beautiful church, a row of old cottages and a small schoolhouse. And to the side of them is the entrance to the works of Webster and Horsfall and Latch and Batchelor.

Hay Mills may take its name from the de la Hays of the Middle Ages, but undoubtedly its fame was established by Victorian manufacturers. In the 1830s the area was part of Yardley in Worcestershire and it was mostly agricultural. There was a tile works by Kings Road, a wharf on the nearby Birmingham to Warwick Canal and that was about it - except for Hay Mills, run by William Deakin a gun barrel maker.

Then a man called James Horsfall became the tenant of the mill. He'd moved from Meriden Street and he was a proper Brummie - a man of ingenuity, skill and inventiveness. Soon after he set up in Hay Mills he went into partnership with the Websters, another family full of craft and endeavour. During the 1850s the company brought out a steel wire that was light, tenacious and 'as hard as glass and as tough as leather'. It could be used for pianos, needles, fish-hooks, springs, small tools, umbrella frames, crinolines and most importantly of all, as rope for engineering, colliery winding gear and ship's rigging.

It was Webster and Horsfall's who supplied wire for the French telegraph cable connecting Marseilles and Algiers, and in 1863 it was this Brummagem manufacturer which stepped into the breach when the Atlantic Cable went dead. Over eleven months, 250 men collared to make 1,600 tons of new cable which was 30,000 miles in length! And this was one that lasted.

An industrial village soon grew up around the factory and in 1863 James Horsfall built school rooms for the children of his workers. Eleven years later he paid for the building of St Cyprian's Church. Over the next 30 years the surrounding fields were cut out with roads filled with terraced tunnel-backs and Hay Mills became a bustling working-class neighbourhood packed with public buildings. There was the 'Adelphi' picture house, a police station and a number of pubs, including the renowned 'Redhill Tavern' which is still emblazoned with the words: "St George he was for England and before he slew the dragon he drank a pint of foaming ale from out a British Flagon."

Through the whole of Hay Mills ran the pulsing artery of 'The Cov', crammed with every kind of shop imaginable. There was Gordon Tay the genial and good-hearted butcher; there was Lacey's the long-established bookie; Miss Hannam was the mouth-watering baker; and Dixon's the pawnbroker took your bundles. There was also the drug store of Miss Winifred Miles, the noted drapery of Bevan's, John Wooton the general merchant and many, many more.

Then in the 1980s, a dual carriageway thundered through Hay Mills and destroyed half the shops. But the neighbourhood refused to be pushed off the map. Webster and Horsfall's is still making quality products as is another major local business, Carter Industries, and the local shopkeepers continue to offer a service to the nearby folk. Hay Mills might be one of Birmingham's smallest districts, but it had a big part to play in making Old Brum the Workshop of the World.

Large crowds watching the elephants cross Hay Mills Bridge, going past Bedder's Fish and Chip Restaurant on the left and towards the 'Plough and Harrow' public house. The circus later took place on the Recreation Ground nearby. (Thanks to Mrs E. Busby whose husband took the photo)

PROUD AND FAMOUS:
SALTLEY

Jet black horses pull the elegant laundaus into the station. As they stop, a footman places a step against the vehicle. With a careful hand, he helps elegantly-dressed ladies out of their carriage. Joined by men in top hats and tails, they saunter towards a train from which steam is beginning to billow. Chattering away, they get on board and enter one of the most luxurious railway dining carriages in the world. Its metal is forged and fashioned by dedicated craftsmen and it is fitted out to the highest standards of quality and workmanship by highly-skilled men, each of whom is talented in a specialised trade. Artfully constructed the carriage is made more impressive by the comfort of the seats and the tastefulness of the decorations.

The party of wealthy folks is embarked on the most romantic and exotic railway journey in the world - the Orient Express. From France they will travel across mountains and remote lands until they reach their destination: Istanbul, still known by many as the fabled Constantinople. And they'll be carried on the way by rolling stock manufactured by the Metropolitan Carriage and Wagon Co. of Saltley, Birmingham!

This name is respected and admired across five continents. And it's not the only celebrated firm in the area - for Saltley also boasts the works of Brown, Marshall and Co., whilst in Washwood Heath there's the Midland Railway Carriage & Wagon Co.

Saltley Bridge (Saltely Viaduct) in the early 1900s. It's either time for clocking on or knocking off by the look of the groups of men and lads – most of whom probably make railway carriages at the nearby Metropolitan Works. It looks as if the photographer is watching from Metropolitan Road on the right, with Crawford Street on the left and some of the fellers cross over towards Nechells. (Thanks to John Marks)

The wedding photo of Eva Gould and Albert Taylor, taken at the rear of Eva's parent's house on the approach from Adderley Road to Saltley Dock, about 1912. It had formerly been the home of William Clayton, of the canal carriers Fellows, Morton and Clayton, before he moved to Castle Bromwich. Eva's dad, Mark (seated on the right), was the foreman at the docks where barges such as the 'Egypt' were made and repaired. He had come to Saltley from Tipton and before that he worked in Dudley. The young girl on the back row is Eva's youngest sister, Mary Ann (Polly). (Thanks to Kathleen Smallwood, daughter of Polly)

Together they're the largest builders of rolling stock in the world. They've got the leading designers and the best workers and their fame increases in the early 1900s when they amalgamate to form the Metropolitan Cammell Carriage and Wagon Co.

It's a remarkable feat for a district to be known from one corner of the globe to another - and it's been achieved in a short time. Until the 1840s Saltley was little more than a hamlet on the east side of a bridge which crossed the River Drea to Duddeston. There wasn't much there, apart from the long-established 'Gate Inn', and most of the land was still owned by Charles Bowyer Adderley, the lord of the manor.

In the whole of Saltley and Washwood Heath there were just 695 people, But the area was ripe for development. It was close to a land-hungry Brum and it was on the main railway line linking the city with Derby. By 1854 Saltley had its own railway station and behind this lay the railway engine works of Joseph Wright. This industrial pioneer had come from London and that's why his firm was later called 'Metropolitan'. By 1862 no fewer than 1,200 men were grafting at its site.

Yet there was more to Saltley than railway carriages. Fellows, Morton and Clayton had their noted boat-building docks off Duddeston Mill Road - and they were overshadowed by the huge gasometers of Birmingham Corporation's Gas Department. Both operations were squashed between the railway line and the Birmingham to Fazeley Canal - and not far away off Bordesley Green Road stood the great factory of the Morris Commercial.

As industry developed so did Saltley, and by the 1880s it was a growing village clustered about its own High Street. Like all villages it had a church, St Saviour's, which was set in fields, and a small school. This had just two classrooms and a hall which was split into three more classes when curtains were pulled across it. But Saltley was soon to lose its rural look. In 1891 it became part of Birmingham and over the next ten years the population of the area increased enormously - from about 9,500 to well over 20,000. From the 'Gate' to Shaw Hill the countryside was banished and a host of new roads covered the land.

By the 1920s Saltley had become a pulsating neighbourhood. It had its own swimming baths in George Arthur Road and cottage baths in Adderley Road. Since 1852 it had boasted a training college at the top of St Saviour's Road, and it also had the services of a small reference library in Adderley Park. Most of all Saltley had its own major shopping centre – the Alum Rock Road and High Street.

What a hive of activity this was! There were pubs and clubs, two picture houses called 'The Rock' and 'The Saltley Grand', churches and chapels, and a variety of national retailers as well as celebrated local shopkeepers such as Jester's.

Saltley Docks and the Morris Commercial have gone and the gas works may soon follow. But 'The Met' continues to provide a firm link with Old Brum. It's still making the best rolling stock in the world, stamped with the proud name - Saltley, Birmingham.

Men of the 204 Battery Medium Field Artillery turning out of Metropolitan Road, the site of the drill hall and heading towards Saltley Viaduct, 1914. This was a territorial unit attached to the nearby Metropolitan Carriage Works. (Information supplied by Mr T. G. Hartle). **The shop on the left is the sub post office and paper shop of Swingler's. Next door is the headquarters of the East Birmingham Labour Party and then the 'Adderley Arm's pub – with Gate Street just past the shops with the canopies. The Ansell's pub on the right is the 'London Tavern', advertising chops and steaks as well as Aston Ales.** (Thanks to Alan Cronshaw)

HISTORY IN THE MAKING:
SMETHWICK

The Great Exhibition of 1851 was the biggest and most impressive event ever held in England. Based in Hyde Park, it was an unrivalled opportunity for manufacturers to show off their ingenuity, innovation and skill at the making of things. No wonder that it was packed with exhibitors from towns and cities across the kingdom. They all wanted to emphasise their own particular talents and they all wanted to stress the contribution made by their own locality to the industrial pre-eminence of Britain. None more so than the leading firms of Brum and the Black Country.

Osler's of Broad Street created an awe-inspiring crystal fountain down which water cascaded, whilst Winfield's of Cambridge Street designed two exquisite brass light fittings which incorporated figurines and which were bought by Queen Victoria and Prince Albert. There were many other celebrated exhibits from West Midlands businesses, but the most impressive contribution of all was the building in which the Great Exhibition itself took place.

Six hundred yards long, it had cost the staggering amount £176,031 and it had taken 1,800 men nine months to erect it. Over 4,000 tons of iron were used in its construction, along with 6,000,000 cubic

Two men surveying the aftermath of the great flood at the top of Cheshire Road, close to the junction with High Street, Smethwick, July 1927. (Thanks to Mrs D. Hill)

Workers at Scribbans cake bakery, Corbett Street, Smethwick – probably during the Second World War.
(Thanks to Mr D. R. Jenkins)

feet of woodwork and 31 acres of sheet glass. And whilst it was sited in London, this Crystal Palace could never have arisen without the talents and abilities of workers from the Staffordshire town of Smethwick. For the ironwork was made by the local operation of Fox Henderson whilst the glass was fashioned by the renowned company of Chance Brothers.

The Great Exhibition was not the first occasion for Smethwick to make its mark in history. In 1796, Matthew Boulton and James Watt had set up the Soho Foundry, where they began to turn out the components for the steam engine which powered so many machines and which were crucial in pushing the world into the industrial age. The building is still there, now home to the well-known weighing machine makers of W. and T. Avery Ltd.

At the dawn of the nineteenth century, apart from Boulton and Watt's factory and a brasshouse, there was little other industrial activity in Smethwick. The greater part of the parish was farmland and most of its one thousand folk grew wheat, barley and potatoes or else they raised cattle. But soon after, manufacturers began to emerge, attracted by the Birmingham Canal which pierced the district and by the availability of large plots of land on which to build modern premises. By the late 1820s, Adkin's and Nock's Soapworks had been set up close to the boundary with Brum, whilst further along the cut and near to West Bromwich could be found Chance's Spon Lane Glassworks.

This firm's global reputation was partly gained because of the expertise of a Frenchman, Georges Bontemp. He taught the local workers how to make sheet glass and later he influenced the move to the manufacture of optical glass. Chance's continued to be an enterprising operation, and by the 1860s it

was also making rolled plate glass and lighthouse lenses. According to an American visitor, Elihu Burritt, the lighthouse department of the factory "will fill the visitor with wonder", for here can be seen "all the working sciences and mechanical forces co-operating in busy harmony". Just think of it - a factory in the middle of England and miles from the sea producing something which saved the lives of countless sailors across the world!

Over 1,700 men, women and children collared at Chance's, and it's obvious that the firm was instrumental in transforming Smethwick from a quiet agricultural district into an industrial boom town. But there were other notable businesses which also played their part in making Smethwick one of the world's greatest manufacturing centres. Over by Cranford Street stood the major factory of Nettlefold and Chamberlain. Later to become part of Guest, Keen and Nettlefold it sent out nuts, bolts and screws to every conceivable place. Then, of course, there was the famous firm of Tangye's. Begun by two brothers in Birmingham, they shifted to Cornwall Road in Smethwick in 1865. Descended from Cornishmen, the men named their factory the Cornwall Works and it was they and their workers who provided the hydraulic equipment which launched the Great Eastern and which raised Cleopatra's Needle on the Thames Embankment.

In recent years Smethwick may have lost its independence, yet no-one should forget either its history or its vital contribution to the making of the modern world.

Queuing to go home after a swim at Rolfe Street Baths, Smethwick, 1950s. Notice the kids with their togs wrapped in their towels and the two young women with their hair done up in turbans. This was a familiar sight in factories with many female workers having to cover their hair for safety. Rolfe Street Baths are now closed but fortunately they are to be dismantled and carefully re-erected at the evocative Black Country Museum.

MELTED IN THE
RAINS OF PROGRESS:
SNOW HILL

We might not be known for our physical features but Brum can hold its own with the best. We've got more canals than Venice and more hills than Rome. Think of it - Rome may boast seven hills, but just add up how many slopes and banks we have just in and around our city centre itself. There's Kingston Hill and Camp Hill, Singer's Hill and Holloway Head, Summer Hill and Newhall Hill, Ludgate Hill and Bennett's Hill - and Snow Hill.

In the Middle Ages it was known as Sandy Lane, because of the type of soil in the area, and although few people lived locally it was a crucial factor in Brum's growth. Our city developed because folk had to pass through Brum at the crossing point of the Rea on their way from London to Shrewsbury and Wales. If they were coming from the south they went up High street Deritend, past the Bull Ring, into High Street Birmingham, along Bull Street and then down Snow Hill. In the other direction, wagons

Looking up Snow Hill from the 'Salutation' on the corner of Summer Lane with the station on the right, 24 June 1959.

Clive Passage, Snow Hill overshadowed by the building of new Brum, 30 November 1960.

and pack horses travelled laboriously from Wednesbury and the rest of the Black Country. They were laden with the coal and iron ore needed to fuel the manufacturers of Brum and to make our famous metal wares.

So great was the movement of raw materials that the traffic wore a hollow way, a deep path, through Snow Hill itself – just as also happened at both Camp Hill and the aptly named Holloway Head itself. By the later 1700s the term Sandy Lane had dropped out of use. No one really knows why but one thing is certain – the change of name to Snow Hill symbolised a transformation in the character of the neighbourhood. To the west the Newhall Estate had been cut out with streets as far as Easy Row, whilst to the east the Gun Quarter had emerged about Weaman Street. And Snow Hill itself was now lined with buildings up to the 'Salutation' bowling green at the corner of Summer Lane.

By the turn of the nineteenth century Snow Hill was a busy and bustling area, but on the night of 18 July 1806 it was the scene of an event which shocked Brummies. A night watchman called Robert Twiford stopped to question someone who was mooching about suspiciously. Twiford was shot dead and a man called Philip Matsell was arrested, found guilty and condemned to hang from the spot of the crime. A gibbet was set up halfway down Snow Hill by Great Charles Street, and 50,000 people gathered to witness the sentence carried out. It was the first execution inside the boundaries of Birmingham.

Within a few years Snow Hill was overwhelmed by more changes. The Great Western Railway decided to construct a major station, opening it in 1852. Unlike the magnificent glass-roofed structure

of the LMS at New Street, the building at Snow Hill was a 'monster wooden shed'. Ugly and ungainly, it was described as much a disgrace to the town as had been the tumbledown buildings which had been demolished to make room for it.

In 1871 the disliked station was torn down and redeveloped. The new building was grand and impressive. It had an attractive entrance with columns in Colmore Row, and from there it stretched the length of Snow Hill, going down almost the whole of the sixty foot slope to Water Street. In total it had platforms running 720 feet, a roof spanning 92 feet and eleven great blue-brick arches - perhaps the most imposing of which is by Lionel Street. In its turn this building has been demolished and replaced - and it is recalled only in a former entrance in Livery Street opposite Cornwall Street. On either side are the letters GWR and above the doorway is a coat of arms with the Latin words 'Domine Dirige nos Virtute et Industrie' 'Lord direct our courage and diligence.'

So much else of old Snow Hill has also disappeared, obliterated by the construction of the Inner Ring Road. It no longer has the Gothic Arcade, the Metropole Theatre, a town sub post office or the Manchester Hotel. Famous businesses have been forced to move away, too - firms like Samuel Thornley and Sons the drysalters, Burroughes and Watts the billiards table makers, Yardleys the musical instrument dealers, Greasley-Norton the confectioners, Frankenburgs the India rubber manufacturers and so many more. Snow Hill may have almost disappeared beneath tarmac and concrete - but nothing can take away its significance to Old Brum.

Snow Hill Station entrance, 1970.

SUBURB GUSHING WITH STREET ACTION:
SPRING HILL

Brum might not be celebrated for its deep, wide rivers but there's plenty of water flowing in our landlocked city. Just think - there's a Well Street in Hockley, a Ladywell Walk up the top end of Hurst Street and a Well Lane across the way from the Bull Ring. And what about those street names recalling water which gushed out of the earth like Spring Road, Tyseley; Spring Lane, Erdington and Spring Vale on the borders of Edgbaston.

There's even two districts named after water sources: Springfield, cornered between Sparkhill, Hall Green and Moseley; and Spring Hill. Shaped like a triangle, this area is cut off from Ladywood by the Stour Valley Railway line, from Brookfields by Spring Hill itself and from Summer Hill by Monument Road. The size of a country village, the neighbourhood's made up of just a few streets: Cope Street, Eyre

It's 10.29 in the morning according to the clock on Spring Hill Library sometime in the early 1900s.

The noted Spring Hill racecourse bookie and publican, Wattie Green, sporting a flower in his button hole outside his pub – the 'Cross Keys' in Steward Street, late 1920s. Wattie was a great pal of Jim Smith, who was famed for his 'Can You Spare A Brown' slogan when raising funds for the Birmingham Mail Christmas Tree Fund. Also in the photo are the Lord Mayor and Lady Mayoress of Birmingham. Alderman Alfred James is holding his billycock (bowler hat) whilst his wife carries a spray of flowers. Years after the gaffer's death, the pub is still known as 'Wattie's'. (Thanks to Denny Green)

Street, Heath Street South, Hooper Street, Ingleby Street, Spring Hill Passage, Springfield Street, Steward Street, Stour Street and the bottom part of King Edward's Road.

Until the early 1800s the locality was mostly fields although two prominent Brummies did live there. One of them was James Turner, whilst the other was a solicitor called George Baker whose grand house was called Springfield. He supported the General Hospital, raised money for many local charities and was a distinguished botanist, but after his death in 1845 his home disappeared and Spring Hill fell under the outpouring of Birmingham.

Within a few years it was packed with working-class folk who collared hard and who were pulled in by a variety of employment. Amongst the bigger factories were Barker and Allen's the makers of German silver, Henry Wilkes the chemical manufacturer and Flynn and Co. the brass founders. Then there were the carriage sheds of the London and North Western Railway Company, a glass works, Albert Phillips the metallic bedstead company, Perry and Castle the packing case maker's and the Safe Beam Lamp company. And we shouldn't forget the importance of smaller businesses like those of Arthur Black the Blacksmith, Bill Landon the sanitary ware supplier, Frank Moseley the motor engineer and Bill Green and Ernie Blaney the chimney sweeps.

Just like any village, Spring Hill had its intimate hucksters' shops and its cosy back-street pubs. Few were more popular than the 'Cross Keys' in Steward Street. Only a little boozer, it was better known as Watty Green's, after the big-hearted licensee who was also a well-respected racecourse bookie. A noted

fund-raiser for the Christmas Tree Fund on every Good Friday, Watty and his wife would hand out 500-odd hot cross buns to the poorer kids of the area.

Spring Hill had so many of its own facilities. It boasted a school which could take in 1036 kids, a railway station, a Municipal Bank, a Billiard Club, a Methodist Chapel and Sunday Schools, and a roller skating rink on the corner of Ingleby Street and Monument Road. And of course it had a stack of shops which crowded the main shopping drag, Spring Hill itself.

Spreading out from the imposing library at the junction of Summer Hill and Icknield Street, every kind of food dealer filled this bustling stretch. There was Verrechia the ice cream maker, Marsh and Baxter the ham and bacon curer, Stoddard the pork butcher, Gibbons the fried fish dealer and Shaw the greengrocer. They were joined by retailers who sold goods and services of every kind imaginable, like Wilkes the chemist, Allibone and Batchelor the hardware dealer, Barrett the corn factor, Dalton the bookie and Minnie Zissman the hatter.

In fact Spring Hill probably had more businesswomen that any other shopping thoroughfare in Brummagem. You could get your hair done by Elizabeth Shore and then get rigged out with a gown from Kay Horton and a pair of shoes from Mrs Riley - and if your funds were too low for that then Nellie Holden the wardrobe dealer would get you sorted. You could buy your drapery from Laura Turberville and fetch your stationary from Edith Perry - while you could get your greens from Violet Wakeling, your groceries from Dorothy Miles, your cooked meats from Mabel Carmichael and your pastries from Blanche Cook. And if you were clammed the dining rooms of Lily Jones, Ida Robinson and Laura Arnold would soon fill you up.

Most of Spring Hill's shopkeepers have gone - along with the folk that made this a thriving Brummie village. But at least you can still borrow books from the library and pop into Watty Green's for a pint. Cheers.

Len Shaw was another well-known and well-liked Spring Hill character, running his greengrocery shop at 111 Spring Hill with his wife, Dorothy.
(Thanks to D. Beasley)

WHAT'S IN A NAME?
STIRCHLEY

When you're having a mooch down the road, watching the traffic pelt along, have you ever wondered what Brum looked like before it was filled with houses, factories and shops. It isn't easy to picture the lay of the land in days gone by, yet we've only got to take note of our place names to bring to mind a vision of the past. Think of the time when a stream ran through Sparkbrook, when Small Heath was a flat piece of shrub land, when trees abounded in Ladywood, when Hodge Hill was a high ground, when Northfield was split up by hedges, and when Hall Green was mostly meadows.

But there are some places whose meanings are more difficult to work out. When we talk about Edgbaston we don't heed that it's the farm (ton) of Ecgbald, nor when we mention Little Bromwich do we recognise that it's a settlement (wich) amidst the yellow flowering shrubs (broom). And when we speak of Harborne little do we realise that it's the muddy (har) stream (borne), or that Hockley is the clearing (ley) in the wood made by Hocca.

Quite a few of Brum's districts have the word 'ley' attached to them. There's Lea Hall and Ley Hill as well as Moseley, Saltley, Shenley, Tyseley, Walmley and Yardley - not forgetting Stirchley, of course.

High Street, Stirchley in the early 1900s, with the Church of the Ascension in the background in Hazelwell Street. On the left, on the corner of Mary Vale Road, is the draper's of David Jones – a firm which traded locally for many years. The shop with the canopy pulled down is the chemist's of Walter Johnson.

A class at Stirchley Street Infants School, 1929. Hilda Pratley is the shy-looking girl fourth from the right in the back row and wearing a tie over her dress. (Thanks to Hilda Pratley)

This district used to be called Strutley and it has the same meaning as Streetly in Sutton Coldfield. Both were clearings by the Roman road of Rycknield Street, which crossed the River Rea at Lifford and passed down what is now the Pershore Road in Stirchley. Then it probably went towards Icknield Street in the Jewellery Quarter before going over the Tame at Perry Barr and on through Sutton Park. By the middle of the 1800s Strutley was becoming known as Stirchley - most likely because a map maker spelt the name wrong!

It was part of Kings Norton in the County of Worcester and was quite a small, triangular-shaped locality. To the east the River Rea cut it off from Hazelwell, whilst on the west the Birmingham to Worcester Canal marked it out from Bournville. Its northern limit was the River Bourne, across which lay its twin neighbourhood of Ten Acres.

Although there was a tube mill at Dogpool and a gun-barrel works on The Fordrough, Stirchley and Ten Acres were overwhelmingly agricultural. Leayhouse Farm clung to the railway line by the modern-day Charlotte Road, whilst Selly Farm stood close to the present junction of St Stephen's Road and Warwards Lane. The whole area was seen as "a favourite country place for weary Brummies having a chance hour to spend on a change of scene".

By the late 1880s Stirchley boasted a post office, a police station, a school, a Methodist Chapel, a railway station and on the Pershore Road a factory belonging to the great screw manufacturers of Guest Keen and Nettlefold. Yet the population remained small, and it wasn't until the end of the Victorian age that urban development began in earnest.

Within a few years many of the fields had fallen before the outpouring of Brum - although Pineapple Farm and Fordhouse Farm survived until after The First World War. The new Stirchleyites had

plenty of local jobs. There was a rubber mill, Clifford's the non-ferrous metals manufacturer, the printing company of Norman Charles, the brass founders of Edwin Showell, Eccles the caravan makers and Cadbury's. The family of chocolate makers weren't just important in providing work, though. They were great benefactors to the whole community. In 1892 they paid for the building of the local Institute, and it was they who gave the land for the Welfare Clinic, the library, and the swimming baths in Bournville Lane.

With these facilities, a variety of pubs and the 'Empire' and 'Pavilion' picture houses, Stirchley and Ten Acres had all the things needed in any town. Yet both had the feel of villages, where everyone was bound together by a selection of shops on the main drag. Stretching from the Dogpool Hotel, past Hazelwell Street to the Rec at Ash Tree Road, the Pershore Road had the lot. Who remembers the appeal of Edward's Stores, the styles at Vanes ladies and gent's outfitters, Quinney's the milliner's and tobacconist's, the mouth-watering cooked meat at Heaton's, and the tasty biscuits of Ida Mary Ladbury. And of course, the district was the base for the famed Ten Acres and Stirchley Co-operative Society.

There's still plenty of cracking retailers down Stirchley, so the next time you traipse down the Pershore Road just think - you're following in the footsteps of Roman legionnaires!

Staff standing proudly outside the grocery store of the Ten Acres and Stirchley Co-operative Society, 1920s.

63

TURNED OUT GRAND FOR PIONEER TISS:
TYSELEY

Warwick Road, Tyseley before 1914. Knights Road is on the left and Tyseley Hill to the right. Notice the fields of Manor House Farm behind the cyclist and back towards Greet. The cycle shop advertising Lucas was owned by Frank Road and next door is Emily Jones the confectioner. Then comes Tyseley Town sub-post office, Miss Louise Aston's drapery is on the corner and George C. Tilley's outdoor across the way.

Who was Tissa and where did he come from? Nobody's got a clue, although his name suggests he was an Anglo-Saxon. Any road, we do know he made his way into the Forest of Arden before or just after the Norman Conquest of 1066. He must have been an adventurous bloke to cleave his way through the trees and bushes that barred his path, but he was obviously spurred on by the need to find somewhere to live.

Tissa took a fancy to a pitch close to where the River Lee rises, nowadays the back of the MEM in Reddings Lane. It wornt much more than a stream, flowing for just a few hundred yards northwards before it joined the River Cole; and nearby was another little river, Rushey Brook - so called because it had plenty of rushes. It must have been tough work making an open space so that he could settle down, raise livestock and till the land. But at last he got it done. Not surprisingly after all his hard collar the place was named after him. It became Tissa's Ley, the clearing of Tissa - or as we call it today, Tyseley.

Harris's Smithy, further along the Warwick Road towards Acocks Green, early 1900s.

There were other pioneers at that time, such as Dudda who made a 'ton', settlement, over Nechells way; and Beorma who built a 'ham', home, for himself and his 'ingas', people, and so started Birmingham. Not far away from Tissa a chap called Bill also hacked out a spot, creating Billesley; whilst even nearer an unknown feller enclosed his space with ditches and banks. It became a 'haeg,' hay - recalled today in Hay Hall. An impressive manor house constructed from the 1300s, this was taken over in 1917 by Reynold's Tubes and was later restored by the company.

For hundreds of years no great events occured in Tyseley, but gradually most of the trees were felled and a number of farms emerged. Manor House, Kings, Stockfield, and Shaftmoor Farms are remembered in modern road names; whilst close to the junction of Holcombe and Ferndene Roads lay Tyseley Farm itself, noticeable for the moat which surrounded it.

A deeply rural area, one of the most important buildings in Tyseley was the smithy of F.G. Harris. Later taken on by Charles Rose, it was next to the 'Britannia' Inn. What a fascinating place this was, where farriers flung hammers, shoes and nails! Filled with horses whinnying, men canting and metal singing, it was lit up by glowering coals, dancing flames and flitting sparks.

As late as 1914 Tyseley remained agricultural, although a small neighbourhood of tunnel back houses had grown up where Knights Road and Tyseley Hill meet the Warwick Road. But after the First World War the look of the area changed swiftly. New roads lined with council houses cut through fields either side of the French-sounding Olton Boulevard West; whilst private housing sprang up between Reddings Lane and the Cole and over by Wharfdale Road.

The new Tyseleyites were served by a cluster of retailers close to the 'Greet Inn' and by a run of shops stretching from Reddings Lane to Tyseley Lane. One of the best known was Oakley's, a traditional grocer who continued to trade until recently. Nearby and still open, as it has been since 1923 is the impressive Tyseley and District Working Men's Club and Institute.

Yet Tyseley was more than a residential district. A great swathe of land was covered by factories and workshops, attracted by the links provided by the main line Great Western Railway which swept through the district. In just Wharfdale Road could be found Smith's Crisps, Stanley Smith and Company the wire drawers, Beckett the Dyers and others. Then there was the Midland Electrical Manufacturing Company making electrical switch gears in Reddings Lane; the Watsonian on the Warwick Road turning out side cars for motorbikes; and the light works plant of the Rover in Hay Hall Road. Not to forget the great Tyseley Engine Sheds, now the site of the Railway Museum; the Public Works Depot in Kings Road; and the huge Tyseley incinerator.

Tyseley doesn't feature regularly in tales of the old end, no songs are belted out about its past and no poems have been written about its people. Yet no Brummie should ignore its importance in making Our Brum the city of a thousand trades. Tyseley may have lost the Bakelite and other firms, but it still has major concerns like Reynold's, the MEM, Harmo, Gabriel's the manufacturer of stainless steel castings, and Dawes the cycle makers. They ensure that Tyseley remains one of Brum's crucial manufacturing areas.

Watsonian side cars and the Tyseley Picture House, between Weston Lane and Boscombe Road, sometime in the 1950s.
(Thanks to Johnny Landon)

WORKERS' HEARTLAND
WINSON GREEN

How big is Brum? Well they used to reckon it was 25 miles just around the Outer Circle 11 route - and Brum today is even greater. It stretches from Sutton Coldfield in the north-east to Frankley in the south-west. That's a lot of square miles. But Brum hasn't always been so large, and it's only in the last 125 years that our city has spread outwards by swallowing up Harborne, Balsall Heath, Saltley, Ward End, Yardley, King's Norton, Erdington and other adjacent towns and villages.

For centuries, Birmingham had more people than these places, but Brummies didn't have much breathing space. They were crammed into a tight area. On the north, our boundary was Hockley Brook, cutting us off from Handsworth and Aston. On the south, Five Ways marked the border with Edgbaston.

To the east, the River Rea separated us from Deritend. And on the west, the approach to the 'Cape of Good Hope' indicated the beginnings of Smethwick.

The whole of old Brum came to just 2,995 acres - and by 1831 there were 142,000 people crowded on to that small space.

Yet not all of that land was built up. Most of Brum's folk were packed into the even more limited district east of Monument Road and Icknield Street.

Spreading out from the Bull Ring, they were gathered densely into old houses and back-to-backs around Digbeth, Hurst Street, Holloway Head, Newtown Row and the Jewellery Quarter.

Beyond Summer Hill and Spring Hill there were few houses, shops and

The bakery and shop of the South family in Heath Street, Winson Green, 1920s.

David J. Jeremy carrying the banner (on the left) as the anniversary parade makes its way down Kitchener Street, 1930s.
(Thanks to David Jeremy)

factories. The area was mostly open land, as at Rotton Park. This had been a hunting ground in the Middle Ages and in the early 1800s it was still countryside.

Across Dudley Road was Birmingham Heath - a flat district covered with shrubs. It was mostly an infertile spot, badly drained and unattractive to farmers. There were only a few inhabitants locally.

One of the best known was Richard Tangye of the famous Smethwick Hydraulic firm, who lived at Winson House. Another was the celebrated Scots innovator William Murdock, the pioneer of gas lighting and an associate of Matthew Boulton and James Watt. Murdock's home was called Ninevah - where Bachus Road now runs. Then there was a house called Bellefield, recalled in a pub of that name in Winson Street, while there was a small village at Winson Green close to Lodge Road.

During the early years of Victoria's reign, Birmingham Heath changed drastically as the waste land was built upon. The first major development came because the town council needed a large site on which to build a borough prison. The most likely spot was at Winson Green - and in 1849 the jail was ready for use. It stood out, not only because of its bulk but also because of its turrets and its general fortress-like appearance. The next year an asylum was opened nearby and in 1852 another major building was erected in the vicinity. This was the hated workhouse, one of the notorious 'bastilles' which haunted the lives of the English poor.

Within a few years this loathed structure was surrounded by streets where working-class people forged strong neighbourhood ties. There were Aberdeen, Carlisle, Lansdowne and Peel Streets - all named after people associated with Lord Aberdeen's government of 1852-5. Then up Winson Green Road there were Wellington and Kitchener Streets, while not far away was Magdala Street, recalling a battle fought in Abyssinia.

But not all of the roads of Winson Green had such distant connections. Piddock Street is deeply rooted in local history and remembers William Piddock, a person who had one of the few farms in the area. When he died in 1728 he left his property to a trust which aimed "to put poor boys out to apprenticeship". In fact, Winson Green jail was built on land owned by Piddock's Charity.

Then there was Perrott Street, called after the man who built Perrott's Folly in Monument Road, and Moilliet Street. This was named after a Swiss merchant whose house was just across the border in Smethwick and who founded a bank which was to merge with Lloyd's in 1865.

By the 1870s, Winson Green was a populous neighbourhood and it had become one of the working-class heartlands of Brum. It was cut through by the canal which brought coal and iron ore from the Black Country. It had wharves and workplaces - like those of Robert Tommas, the maltser, and the British White Lead Company. It was pierced by a railway which joined us with Wolverhampton and it had its own station. It had two main roads - the Dudley Road and Lodge Road - as well as two large churches, the Anglican St Cuthbert's and the Catholic St Patrick's. It had chapels and missions, schools and shops. Most of all, it had people. Thousands of people from England, Ireland, Wales and elsewhere. They were the people who transformed the waste land of Birmingham Heath into the thriving neighbourhood of Winson Green.

Josephine Clarke (centre) and her husband Ernest (behind) thanking neighbours in and about Perrott Street who'd offered them furnishings, fittings and money after a fire destroyed the ground floor of their house, 4 October 1974. Josephine is shaking hands with local grocer Joe Eccles who offered the couple accommodation in an empty house he owned in Eva Road.

HAVING
FUN

ON YER BIKE

"How much y'got?" The two other lads push their hands deep into their pockets, shuffle them around and bring them back out. Palms upturned, they show off their coins. One's got a farthing, the other a ha'penny. "Smashing!" says the leader. "Just enough. I've got three farthings, so we can get some rocks and still tek out a bike."

Chuffed with themselves, they run into the huckster's to get their cuckooks, rush out and speed down the street – chucking their flat caps at each other, and making sparks fly with the nails in the heels of their boots. Down at the bottom there's a house that's slightly bigger than the rest, with a bit of a yard at the side. Outside hangs a wooden board emblazoned with the words 'Bikes For Hire'. They push the door open and see the owner of the shop in the corner, surrounded by a couple looking at three crocks, intent on making a good bike out of them.

A cycling club ready for the off just before the First World War. Albert Parsons from Bertha Road, Greet is fourth from the left. On his left is his wife, Miriam Esther (Hetty), who was born a Deakin and came from Lee Road, Greet. On Albert's other side is his sister and his brother is second from the right. Albert and Hetty married in 1911 and lived all their married life in Bertha Road, whilst Albert always cycled to work and to the allotments in Springfield Road. (Information supplied by Joan Guggiani, a daughter of Albert and Hetty)

W. E. Luke with his bike and ready for work at the sub post office in Anderton Road, Sparkbrook, 1923. Aged fifteen, his wage was eleven shillings a week. (Thanks to W. E. Luke)

"Can we have a bike for an hour mister?" The man looks up, his face streaked with oil and his hands black as coal. "Give us your tuppence then." The cheekiest lad passes over the money. "Mind y're back in an hour – or else y'll cop out! And don't all three on y'gerron it at once. D'y hear me!"

Too late. They're out in the street with their 'sit and beg' bike with its flat handlebars and almost treadless tyres. The big 'un sits astride the saddle and the quickest of the other two balances himself sideways on the cross bar – while the one who lost out runs beside them.

For over an hour they ride around the streets – the flattest ones wherever possible – standing up to pump the pedals and then sitting back down and free-wheeling for a few seconds. They haven't got a watch but they're well over their time. So they hurry back to the bike man's street, and wait till an innocent looking lad comes along. "Ere are mate. Do us a favour, we've got to get home quick. Tek back this bike for us?"

And the unsuspecting kid pushes the cycle down to the yard where its owner is waiting, getting more and more angered as he watches the seconds tick on his battered old alarm clock.

Then, as they get older and start work, the thoughts of the lads turn to getting their own bikes. No chance of buying one outright, but if your dad'll sign for you then you can get one on the drip. If not, you can try to save up enough to get a second-hand bike from a mate or out of adverts in The *Mail*.

Such opportunities opened for you once you had your own bike! In the light nights you could have a ride to Earlswood Lakes, going past the old mill at Trittiford and then down to the Ackerdocks before

you reached your goal. Or perhaps you might go out to the blue bells at Chelmsley Wood, or else to the Lickeys or even to the lakes at Kingsbury. Then on a Sunday you could plan on a longer trip. Dressed in your top and shorts with a bottle of water and some sandwiches you'd set off with your mate at about 10 in the morning – heading for Stratford, Hagley, Malvern, Tamworth or one of a host of other places.

This week the destination's Coleshill. Down the Cov Road you go, up past the newly developing Sheldon and out to Bickenhill. Then turn at the island and along to that pretty town above the River Cole. What a feat if you could cycle all the way to the top of the hill – and then perhaps you were ready for the biggest challenge of all, Liveridge Hill on the other side of Henley.

Hair blowing in the wind, the sounds of birds singing, the smell of fresh air, the sight of open spaces – a heady mix when you come from the overcrowded city where factories belch out smoke and stinks and where green is almost an unknown colour. You join hundreds of others with the same idea of getting out to the countryside, and you could always pick out those in a cycling club because they'd have racers and would be pedalling faster than anyone else. Head down, shoulders hunched and feet pumping up and down furiously – you could even imagine you were the famous racer, Tommy Godwin! And if you were lucky you might keep pace with a couple of girls, who you could shout across to and who you might see again. See you on the road next week!

Eighteen-year-old Reginald Upson with his older brother's new bike on the corner of Upper Webster Street and Parliament Street, Aston 1949. (Thanks to Reginald Upson)

FOOTBALL CRAZY

It's early in the evening and summer has just burst into life. In the hazy blue sky, the sun shines bold and strong. Its light forces a way through gloomy entries and dark double-knacks, finds a path between tottering chimney stacks and towering spires, and seeks a route via gaps in the rooftops. Brightness is shafted on to the streets, pressing back the shadows. A few old-timers stand canting on the doorstep, and one or two have pulled chairs on to the footpath. Some of the big wenches are skipping, a gang of lads is playing cricket and the little 'uns are chasing each other, shouting out 'ackey-one-two-three!'

Down at the end of the street, there's a bomb peck which has been cleared and flattened and a small crowd has gathered to watch a kick-about. Well, it might look like a kick-about to an outsider who's just passing by, but to those who are in the know it's much more than that – it's a back-street international! One street's tekking on the next and this is a serious game. No tin cans or pig's bladders blown up 'cus someone's copped hold of a caser! A real leather case-ball, dark and tanned, with laces holding it

The Aston Villa team that won the English Cup, 1904-5. Standing: G. B. Ramsay (secretary); F. Miles; H. Toney, director; H. Spencer, captain; F. W. Rinder, chairman; W. George, goalkeeper; J. Devey, director; and J. Grierson, trainer. Seated: D. V. A. Jones, director; W. Brawn; W. Garratty; H. Hampton; J. Bache; A. Hall; and J. T. Lees, director. Front: J. Pearson; A. Leake; and J. Windmill

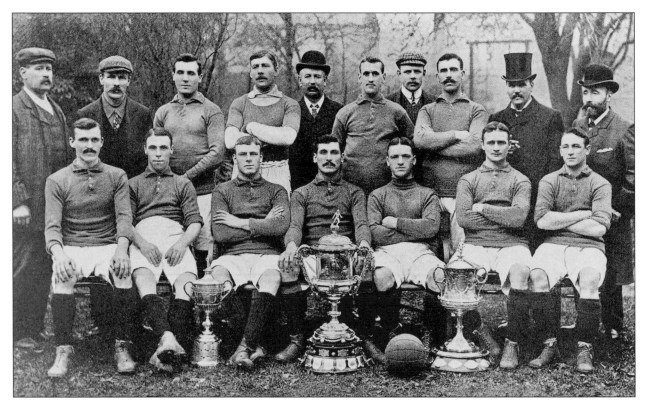

Birmingham Football Club (later Birmingham City) team and officials, 1905-6. Back row: Simms, assistant trainer; Norman, trainer; Glover; Robinson; W. Adams, president; Stokes; Howard; Dougherty; Dr. Stanley; Alfred Jones, secretary. Front row: Beer; Green; Mounteney; Wigmore; W. H. Jones; Wilcox; Field.

together and dubbined to waterproof it and to mek it softer! It's the kind of ball you only dreamt about playing with, the kind of ball you wished for each Christmas knowing all the time that you'd got no chance of getting one.

Any road, here it was, a caser. A couple of blokes have picked out the length and width of the pitch, and have done the same for the goals. Jerseys have been chucked down in four bundles to make the posts and there's even a chap who's offered to act as a referee. No messing about, this match has to be played properly – even if the lads have no kit and even if they are running about in pumps or boots.

There's some good players. There's fellers who can dribble so delicately it seems the ball is hanging on to their toes and there's a couple of good stoppers who try to mek sure nothing gets past them. There's an agile goalie who darts hither and thither, and a strong tackling left back. There's an elegant wing half, a stylish inside right and two strapping centre forwards.

At every chance they thrust their powerful bodies forward, ready to fasten on to the slightest opportunity and to slide in with their legs outstretched or to stiffen their neck muscles and hit the ball firmly with their foreheads. Yet for all the talent and ability, not one of them is himself.

Each of them has a favourite player who's grabbed their attention and who is their other self – and it's these men who are really playing on that peck in the back streets of Old Brum. The right winger's the lively Leslie Smith of the Villa but he's got some stiff opposition from Johnny Hancocks of the Wolves. At inside right there's the highly-rated Bobby Robson of the Baggies, and behind him he's got the up and coming Don Howe – although there's a lot of support for another full back, the mighty Stan

'The Wham' Lynne who's one of the hardest hitters of a ball in the game.

There's only one choice for goalkeeper. It has to be the great Gil Merrick of the Brummagem. He's got plenty more of the Blues lads with him 'cus there's Gordon Astall and Jeff Hall who've both been picked for England and there's also the fast-running Eddie Brown and Peter Murphy, the scorer of a spectacular semi-final goal.

Not to be outdone, the Villains have got their following for the Geordie Gentleman Johnny Dixon, the Irish international Peter McParland and for Vic Crowe and Jimmy Dugdale.

But the local stars aren't the only ones who're showing their deft touches and keen tackling 'cus there's an army of world-class footballers on view. There's Tommy Lawton and Dixie Dean, there's 'Wor' Jackie Milburn and Tom Finney, there's Duncan Edwards and Stanley Matthews. You name 'em and they're there!

A bit of waste-ground in a tough part of Brum. It doesn't seem much but take a closer look and something special will reveal itself. You'll not only see talented kids playing football but also you'll see lads behaving like sportsmen. There's no swearing at the referee, there's no violence by the spectators, there's no nastiness or vileness by the players. They're playing the most beautiful game in the world and they're playing it with passion, pride and respect. They're hard and forceful but they're fair and sporting.

Football came from the back streets of cities like Old Brum and it has spread across the globe and captured the imaginations of millions. And why? Because it is the people's game. You can play it anywhere and any place. You don't need fancy equipment and the smallest player on the park can be the best. It's the greatest gift given to the world by the working-class folk of industrial Britain, and while the game of football is played then the back-street internationals should never be forgotten.

What's the score? Well it was a tight match, it flowed one way and ebbed the other, first one side held the advantage and then the other. I'll let you know next week!

Belgrave, one of the many pub-based teams, 1932-3. This one met the 'Belgrave', Belgrave Road Highgate. Seated second from the right is Billy Newbold, who later became the street bookie in Hick Street. Our Grandad Perry is standing second from the left and his brother Harry is standing second from the right. Grandad also came out of Hick Street. He was a choir boy at St Alban's and went to Upper Highgate Street School. When he was fourteen Our Grandad was chucked out of his house by his dad who was very cruel to them. After sleeping a night in the Rowton House he was taken in by Mr Fields, a kindly local policeman, and lived with them till he married Our Nan.
(Thanks to Trevor Newbold).

THE MONKEY RUN

A hint of smile on her lips, she looked up from her sewing and fastened her eyes on the teenage girl. For at least a quarter of an hour she'd been standing in front of the little mirror on the mantlepiece, brushing her hair, fiddling with her fringe and huffing and puffing as she did so. Her mom couldn't help but say something. "The way you're going, you'll brush y'r hair out, ma girl. And then where'll y'be."

The youngster shifted her gaze to the older woman. "If our dad let me have it cut, then I wouldn't have to keep on brushing it before I went out." That's true, thought her mom, and goodness knows her'd nagged the life out of him to try and get round him. But he wornt having none of it. The kids were right when they moaned that he was a bit of a Victorian. Still, he meant well and he thought the world of his girls. "It don't mek no difference y'gooing on. Y'know he wunt let yer ave it cut. Any road, what's all this brushing for? Yer gorra a bloke?"

The Lozells Road, looking from Lozells Street west towards Villa Cross, just before the First World War. Scott's, the domestic machinery dealers, occupies three one-storey shops, with the Lozells Post Office next door, alongside which is a branch of George Mason's, the grocer. Scott's shops were later taken over by Jackson's the house furnishers and England's the boot and shoe makers.

"No", was the quick answer. "I'm just gonna goo for a mooch down the Cov with a couple of me pals. That's all." Putting the brush on the sideboard, the teenager pulled her frock down at the sides and checked that her shoes looked polished. At last she was ready and with a "mek sure you're back before ten!" from her mom "Or else you'll cop it!" she was through the door and gone.

She almost ran down the yard and through the entry to meet up with her pals on the corner. All set, they went off down Little Green Lane. When they got to the bottom they linked arms and started their walk up the Cov.

Canting and giggling as they went, now and then they yelled across the horse road to another group of girls they knew. Then a pair of lads came towards them, one of them swaggering and all full of himself. As he went by he 'click-clicked' at them and gave them a wink. They wornt having no cotter with him. Their moms'd 'ave a blue fit if they had - and you never knew if one of the neighbours was about, ready to run back with tales. Flinging their heads into the air and thrusting their shoulders forward, they carried on regardless. Behind them the cheeky one shouted something about them being toffee-nosed. They took no notice, having a titter to theirselves when the lads were out of earshot.

Laughing and messing about, they tripped on their way. Crossing Grange Road and then Watts Road they stopped for a few minutes outside the 'Coronet' Picture House, telling each other they'd meet there tomorrow for a night at the flicks. Mind you, they daynt hang about for long 'cus they knew if a copper seen them they'd be moved on or even given a good telling off. They'd even heard of some

'The Cov', Coventry Road, early 1900s. On the right is William Green the bootmaker, Arthur Lewis the tailor, and Miss Lucy Brooks the fancy draper. The shop with the ladder against it is that of Horatio George Turner, corn dealer, whose family occupied the same premises for many years and who still sell agricultural supplies on the Cov. Across the way, on the corner of Regent's Park Road, stands the branch of the Midland Bank and Neal's the dentist – both long-standing businesses locally.

Down the 'Main', Soho Road, Handsworth, during the inter-war years. On the corner of Murdock Road can be seen Purus Bakeries, and next but one is the eye-catching 'Red Lion' pub. In the distance, the clock tower of the old Handsworth Council House can just be picked out.

wenches who'd been pinched 'cus they'd been singing as they went up the monkey run. You couldn't believe it, youngsters who weren't harming no-one and they weren't even allowed to gather on the main drag without a palaver.

Then it was off again, going across Muntz Street and heading towards the 'Gondola Milk Bar' where they were going to pop in and have a drink. They never made it. A couple of chaps came into view. They knew them slightly and as they reached each other, the one lad accidentally on purpose nudged his mate into the three girls. Going all red, he stammered he was sorry and with his mucker mouthing at him, 'Goo on,' he bashfully asked one of the girls could he walk with her up to the park. "But what about me pals," she blurted out, hoping they'd say, "Oh goo on. We're alright. Goo with 'im and we'll meet up with yer in a bit." Good as gold they did.

That was it. Up to Victoria Park they walked and then back down again to Green Lane where her friends were waiting for her. Heart beating and her tummy doing gambols, she waited for him to say 'tara'. He was just as nervous. As she turned to go, he mustered all his confidence and called out "Can I tek y'the pictures tomorra?" He felt sick with the collywobbles, but when she said "Yes" he could have floated all the way home. It had been a cracking night down one of the monkey runs of Old Brum!

A BOSTIN SUNDAY SIGHT:

BOYS' BRIGADE

Sundays were so different to the rest of the week. Fewer vehicles trundled down the streets. Less folk traipsed along the footpaths. Most shops were closed. Factory bulls didn't hoot. Machinery didn't shudder. It seemed as if the whole world had called 'barley!' and wanted to have a short break in the hurry-scurry of normal life.

Yet Sundays weren't hushed altogether. Church bells pealed. Newspapers rustled. Taters and veggies boiled while roasts hissed. Periwinkle men, barrel organ players and ice-cream sellers plied their trade. Gaffers shouted 'Time gentlemen please!' at 2 o'clock in the afternoon. And everywhere wirelesses were tuned in for the crackling voices of Two-Way Family Favourites, bringing with them news of BFPO.

But the most distinctive sound of Sunday had to be the blaring of the bugles and the banging of the drums of the bands of the Boys' Brigades. It seemed that they were in every part of Brum. You'd hear the strains in the distance and gradually the music would get louder until it burst out in full blast as the company marched down your end. There was always a medley of kids in their Sunday best milling around the band -'cus that was about all that you were allowed to do on the day of rest. And very often a little bunch of them would gigglingly sing 'Here comes the Boys Brigade, all covered in marmalade'.

What a bostin sight they made, those lads of the band. Each had an eye-catching white belt, stretching diagonally downwards from his right shoulder and throwing into relief the darkness of his

The Digbeth Brass Band of the Boys' Brigade, early 1900s (Thanks to Helen James).

The Lord Mayor of Birmingham, Councillor Mrs Freda Cocks, and the president of the Birmingham battalion of the Boy's Brigade, Harold Burnett, are with some of the eleven local members who won the Queen's Awards in 1978, 6 March 1978. The awards were gained through service to the community and to the Brigade. Four of the winners came from churches at Longbridge and another four from Solihull.

top and trousers. Everything was held in place by a wide belt and glistening buckle. But the most outstanding feature was the dark pill-box cap with two white braids, a chin strap, the company number on the front and a white button on top. Of course, each cap was angled jauntily on the right side of a lad's napper.

The smartest figure of all was the officer who led the march. Like a Scottish highlander he wore a glengarry, a cap pointed at the front which had a BB badge on the left side and a couple of ribbons at the back. His suit was dark, his collar white and starched, his tie black, his gloves tan and his short stick was brown.

As he led his lads proudly down the street, they were watched by blokes leaning through windows and women standing on doorsteps. For a few minutes the Sunday calm was broken by a wave of noise and movement. Then it was gone, along with its hangers-on. Folk went back inside as the tune became fainter. Once again the street was hushed - at least until next Sunday.

The soldierly look of the Boy's Brigade had been designed deliberately by William Smith, who'd founded the movement in Glasgow in 1883. He was keen that teenagers should have something positive to do on an often-boring Sunday. So he came up with the idea of 'Drill and Discipline'. He formed a band of volunteers who received religious instruction and a military-style training but who also took part in games and activities.

The object of this Boys' Brigade was clear: 'The advancement of Christ's Kingdom among Boys and the promotion of habits of Obedience, Reverence, Discipline, Self-respect and all that tends towards a true Christian manliness'. It was an objective taken up eagerly throughout Britain and by 1902 there were so many companies in Brum that they formed a battalion of their own.

Many men have devoted their lives to the principles and activities of the Boys' Brigade in our city - perhaps none more devotedly than Harold Burnett. Starting with the 10th Birmingham Company attached to the Moseley Road Methodist Church he rose through the ranks and became President of the Birmingham Battalion in 1965. Holding the title for 14 years he then became Honorary President.

During the centenary year of the Boys' Brigade in 1983 he held fast to the conviction that a movement so popular in Old Brum still had a meaning today. The reason was simple. The Boys' Brigade was "voluntary because all can join, compulsory because we expect a high standard of behaviour and discipline". Lets hope it continues to thrive and instill its principles.

1,500 members of the Boys' Brigade taking part in the annual church parade of the Birmingham Battalion 22 May, 1978. The service took place at Central Hall and was attended by two former members: John Sever, Labour MP Ladywood; and Reginald Eyre, Conservative MP for Hall Green.

HORSES FOR COURSES:
BROMFORD BRIDGE

"Six to four the field! Six to four the field!" cried the bookie with the distinctive language of his trade. Standing on his stool in line with other bookmakers, he was determined to grab the ears of the punters who were milling about the betting ring, seeking the best deal for the horse they fancied.

Gradually he drew in a huddle of punters, who gazed at the list of runners with their prices scrawled in chalk on a blackboard alongside.

Now and then someone would stretch forward, silver coins in one palm, and whisper to the bookmaker while nodding up towards the name of the chosen horse. Taking the money in one hand, with the other the bookie thrust out a ticket to the punter who was already stepping back into the muddle of racegoers.

Lord Willoughby de Broke toasting success to the long bar at Bromford Bridge after the new refreshment buildings had been opened by the Lord Mayor of Birmingham, Alderman Donald Johnstone.

Sitting on the weighing in scales at Bromford Bridge.

It was as if silence had been banished from the whole course. Everywhere people were chatting and yapping, and here and there tipsters paced up and down, beckoning buyers with their bold claim: "I've got a tip! I've got a tip!" It was a confusing and complicated scene, but it suddenly became ordered and simple when the horses came under starter's orders. For a few seconds there was a hush and stillness, ended abruptly by a great roar as the horses pounded forward from the starting gates. All eyes were dragged to the silken-clad jockeys hunched over their mounts. A cacophony of voices battered the sky.

Punters urged on their fancy, berated a horse which threatened their bet, and cursed and cajoled the riders, while the bookies mouthed unspoken words that were just as eloquent for all that they were unuttered. As the smooth and shiny animals sped past the winning line, some folk thrust their arms upwards in triumph whilst others tore up their betting tickets in disgust.

And so it went on, race after race, meeting after meeting. But this race at 9.30pm on June 21st, 1965, was different. It was the last to be run on Brum's own racecourse, Bromford Bridge. The victorious horse was Welshman, ridden by Greville Starkey. Fittingly the earlier Bromford Handicap Plate had been won by the aptly-named favourite Selly Oak, with Lester Piggott as its jockey.

Like all other town courses, Bromford Bridge was losing popularity. The crowds seemed to prefer the smaller, almost rural meetings at places like Warwick and Stratford. Certainly Brum's racecourse was different to these prettier spots. On one side was the railway, and just beyond loomed the great works of Fort Dunlop which daily sent out the whiff of rubber. Nearby were the Bromford Wire Mills and it wasn't all that far to the Wolseley car factory in Drews Lane. But if it was mostly industrial to the north

and west, then to the south were strung out neat residential roads, whilst to the east lay Castle Bromwich Gardens and the remnant of an agricultural past.

Still, even if it wasn't set in fields, then Bromford Bridge was a fine racecourse; in fact, it was one of the best in England. The flat course had easy bends, and from the last turn into the straight there was a smashing four and a half furlong run which allowed the jockeys plenty of time to balance their mounts and challenge at the right moment. And the steeplechase course was just as good, letting the riders stay on the rails throughout and giving them a good chance to take a measure of the fences.

All this mattered no longer. At 9.40pm more than 9,000 people watched Lord Willoughby de Broke, chairman of the racecourse directors, hand over the finishing post to Councillor Bond, chairman of the city housing committee. Just under a year later work began on building an estate of 1,900 homes. At a time of housing shortage, the new properties were badly needed and soon 7,500 people lived on the former racecourse.

But if the end of racing was a good thing for many, it was a sad occasion for Francis Ford, the clerk of the course whose grandfather had opened Bromford Bridge in 1895. It was just as sad for Reginald Stonebridge, who'd been head groundsman for 34 years; for Hal Walker who'd been a bookie at Bromford since 1924; and for 'Auntie' Mabel who'd been working in the longest bar in the world for forty-odd years. Bromford Bridge: a name which reminds us of the time when Brum had its own racecourse.

'Naval Officer' refusing to go into the stalls at Bromford Bridge, 25 February 1964.

HIGH DAYS
AND
HOLIDAYS

A CHRISTMAS WISH BY THE PEOPLES' WRITER:
DICKENS AT THE TOWN HALL

As he opened the door a rush of coldness swept into the room, dragging with it big flakes of snow. Pounding his feet, he took off his coat and stepped close to the fire. Almost breathing in the warmth, he cut off a twist of baccy and pushed it into his clay pipe. Stooping down he let the flames lick at a thin bit of paper and lit his smoke. One elbow on the mantelpiece, he took a puff and then moved over to the little recess on the left of the black-leaded range.

Stretching his hand toward a shelf he picked up a magazine and shifted to sit on a squab alongside. Once he was comfortable he began to read. In a room illuminated by only an old-fashioned lamp he struggled to catch sight of the words, yet never once did it strike him to put the story down – so strongly was he pulled into the tale.

Now and then he chuckled, occasionally he sighed and sometimes he murmured a word that was hard to catch. At last he reached the end of the instalment, but the enjoyment of the read wasn't over. As she always did, his wife looked up from her darning and mouthed an almost silent "well?" at him.

The Town Hall during one of the triennial music festivals. (Thanks to Len Taylor)

The Town Hall in the early 1900s. Notice the young lad pushing the basket carriage, and the Chamberlain water fountain in the background.

That was his cue to recount the story, relishing a chance to become part of the plot – something he'd do again tomorrow with some of his mates at work.

Only one writer in the land had such an effect, entrancing hundreds of thousands of ordinary folk. His name? Why, it could only be Dickens, the people's writer, the man who wrote about them – the landladies and inn keepers, the clerks and shopkeepers, the factory workers and labourers, the homeless and dispossesed and so many more.

Comically, tragically and realistically he brought to the fore the lives of his own, the people from whom he sprang and whom he never forgot, no matter how wealthy he became. Through the success of his works he strove to expose injustice, he sought to reveal deprivation, and he battled to lay open to the world the hardships and hard times endured by so many. No wonder that the people flocked to hear him when he toured the country giving readings from his works, like they did that Friday, December 30th, 1853, when he walked on to the stage of our Town Hall here in Brum.

It was the third night that he'd done so, in a goodhearted gesture to raise funds for the proposed Birmingham and Midland Institute. On the 27th he'd read from *A Christmas Carol*, on the 29th from *The Cricket on the Hearth* and on both occasions the magnificent building was packed with expectant listeners.

But that third night the atmosphere was even more charged for this was the most special evening of them all. This was the night on which Dickens had asked that the price of admission should be reduced so that the working people of Brum could afford to come inside. Paying a tanner entry, they crammed the Town Hall – buttonmakers and jewellers, navvies and hawkers, smiths and toolmakers,

washerwomen and sempstresses and a host of others representing virtually every occupation in this the city of a thousand trades.

Chattering excitedly with anticipation, they kept their gaze steadfastly at the front, for not one of them wanted to miss the appearance of Dickens. No fanfare announced him, but as soon as he came forward the great gathering fell silent. Dickens was not a tall man, yet he dominated that massive room, every face pulled to a head that was balding and bearded and from which the eyes shone strongly. Then, as if moved by a hidden hand the assembled working people of Brummagem stamped their feet and clapped their hands in salute to their author.

Holding a folder, inside which was *A Christmas Carol*, he moved to a lectern – but before he began he spoke directly to his 'good friends'. He told them that he had been animated by two desires when he'd asked that the main body of the audience be composed of working men and their families. He'd wished "the great pleasure of meeting you face to face at this Christmas time, and accompany you myself through one of my little Christmas books". But also he wanted the opportunity of stating publicly his earnest hope that the Institute would recognise one great principle – "that the working man shall, from the first to the last, have a share in the management of an institution which is designed for his benefit".

Then Dickens moved on to his reading, impassioned by the enthusiasm of his listeners. When he finished, it was declared "one of the finest things, without exception, ever seen in that hall". A vote of thanks was passed with a resounding "aye" after which a working man called out for three cheers for Charles Dickens and another three for Mrs Dickens. The noise swept across the room, echoing to and fro. When it calmed, Dickens wished everyone "many happy returns of this great birthday time, and many prosperous years". What better wish for us all at Christmas?

The music festival at the Town Hall on 10 October 1917. Thomas Beecham is conducting and Neville Chamberlain, a Lord Mayor of Birmingham and later Prime Minister, is standing on the rostrum third on the right.

HAPPY AT THE REZZER AND THE VALLEY

It was the summer holidays and the streets belonged to the kids. Cans were kicking, boots were scuffing, ropes were skipping, legs were jumping. Whips were topping, marlies were shooting and fingers were flicking. From one corner to another kids were darting, scurrying, larking and mooching.

From one end to the next there rang out cries of "acky-one-two-three!", "pass it!", "sheep sheep come over!", "pack it up!" and "barley". In the middle of the helter skelter stood a knot of older wenches. Arms folded under their busts, they took no notice of the shouts and the scampering and just carried on yapping away. "Where you gooing f'y're olidees?", said the one and the others threw each other a quick look, knowing that she was determined to tell them all where she was off to. "Cuz Our Dad sez we're gooin' to Weston!"

The others piped up one by one. "We might goo to Rhyl, if we're lucky". "We're gooin' to Our Nan's in Wales". "Our Mom's sez she'll tek us fer a day to Our Auntie's in Evesham". "Our Dad promised us he'll tek us for a ride or two". "We're gooin on picnic."

Mr Goodridge in his bathing suit outside the corrugated bungalow he shared with two friends. He and his wife did their courting at Happy Valley, Yardley Wood in the summer of 1921. (Thanks to Mrs Goodridge).

Boaters on the Stratford-on-Avon Canal at Happy Valley, not far from Christ Church and Warstock Farm, probably 1920s.
(Thanks to Audrey Stokes whose parents and uncle and aunt owned one of the weekend chalets/bungalows at the valley).

They'd all spoken bar one, and there was an embarrassed silence as their eyes turned to the girl who hadn't opened her mouth. "Jus cus Our Mom's a widder, they think we ain't gooin' nowhere. Well I'll knock the bob off 'em," she thought. "We're gooin' away, an all!" She almost threw the words at them. Her mates gazed at her, not really believing her. "We're gooin' to Little Blackpool! And we're gooin' to Happy Valley. Cus Our Mom sez why bother spending money on trips somewhere else when y've got all you want in Brummagem!"

The next day she got up early, determined to give her mom a rest and to show her mates she was having a holiday.

The lads ran down the yard and delved into the miskins until they found a couple or three jam jars, around the top of which they put a bit of string so they could carry them. Then they fetched an 'a'penny cane and attached to it a line of black cotton. They'd got their rod and line, and summat to put the fish in. Now all they needed was some bait, and they'd find that on the banks of the Rezzer where they could dig for worms.

All set. Our Wench got 'em all together and marched them off from Hope Street. Up Sun Street, Lea Bank Road and Islington Row to Five Ways they went, and down the posh Hagley Road to that big hotel, the Plough and Harrow. Then along Waterworks Road, past that strange tower that gave its name to Monument Road and at last to their goal – "Birmingham Blackpool Week" at Edgbaston Rezzer!

thousands of people walking about, and many of them were heading for Pat Collins's fun fair. That was too dear for the little group, but they had a bostin' day anyway.

The two lads sat at the water's edge, determined to catch Jack Bannocks or Sticklebacks, while the big 'un took the other pair to listen to the music and for a walk. What a day they had! But at last it was time to go home and moaning and groaning the kids set off behind their big sister. But she hadn't finished with her treats. She collared and scratted until the week before school she'd got enough money for another holiday.

This time she took them to the Happy Valley, up past Kings Heath. They had to catch the tram there, getting off at Alcester Lane's End and then they traipsed up to the cut and the fair. The kids were clammed and thirsty – but she'd got a real treat for them.

She fancied doing things properly, so they got in the little boat and went across the canal to the row of cottages on the other side. One of them had got a few tables outside. She sat the kids down, ordered some tea, pop and cakes and as they scoffed it, she sat back chuffed with herself.

"You know, Our Wench," said one of the kids. "You're the best in the world. Who'd have thought we'd have had two holidays in Brummagem – at the Rezzer and the Happy Valley?"

Miss E. Simpson and her niece making sandcastles at Edgbaston Reservoir during Blackpool week, probably early 1950s.

DRESSED TO THE NINES FOR MAY DAY PARADE

Birmingham was one of the world's largest cities. It resounded to the clamour of manufacture. It smelled of the making of things. It was made smoky by its industries. But in the midst of the hustle and bustle of a great city, the countryside was not forgotten.

Long-established agricultural customs remained strong, simply because Birmingham was filled mostly with people who had their roots in the villages of Warwickshire and Worcestershire. They remembered the traditions taught them by their mothers, fathers and grandparents. They made sure that the celebrations of the rural past were still popular in an urban setting. And they continued to hold up age-old festivals like May Day.

Remember dinner time on May Day? The kids have come home from school. They've had something to eat and now the moms are calling the wenches over to them. As they're dressing them in white frocks made for the occasion, there's a knock at the door. It's one of the women neighbours. She's been making

Girls in Icknield Port Road, Ladywood with garlands of spring flowers in their hair and ready to dance round the Maypole, 1923. (Thanks to Doreen Draisey who was too young to take part in the festivities).

Peter, the horse in the centre, won first prize in the May Day procession of Randall Bros and Parsons, fruit merchants at Smithfield Market, probably 1920s. Ginger on the right and Darkie on the left dead-heated for second place.

garlands for all the kids of her yard. The flowers are daisies, bound together gently and intricately to make an attractive chain which looks like a bridesmaid's head-dress.

Togged up in their finery, the girls go back to school. Some teachers have carried the Maypole outside and placed it on the horse road. It's decorated in colourful ribbons, which hang down from the top of the pole and which make fascinating patterns in the air as the wind blows them.

Other teachers have dragged the piano into the street. One of them starts to play a tune. There are moms and neighbours on the pavement. They watch as small groups of girls take it in turns to dance around the Maypole, weaving carefully through the darting ribbons. When the dancing is finished, one of the children is chosen as the May Queen.

The wenches are not the only ones to be done up. Early in the morning, the delivery men have cleaned their carts and got them spick and span, making sure that the signs of their firms look especially good. They've polished their horse brasses and hung them on their large, dignified-looking shires. They've darkened the hooves of their animals with black lead; they've brushed them and combed them; they've hung bells from their heads; and they've attached rosettes to them. More than that they've plaited their tails at the top, and they've entwined their manes with flowers and ribbons.

Then at breakfast-time, the wives of the carters add the finishing touches to the display. A big leather collar, shaped like an upside down "U" rises from the flanks of the horse and above its head. It's covered in flowers, beautifully arranged. The carter puts fresh clobber on, perhaps with a leather pinny, and places his hat on his head. It might be a billycock, or a trilby or a flat cap - it all depends on his job. Now they're ready, and the parading of the streets can begin.

What a sight! Cart after cart doing the rounds of Brummagem. So many firms are represented. There's the brewers' drays of Ansells and Davenports. Over there are the milk floats of the Co-op and the Midland Counties Dairies. Across the way are the delivery wagons of the railway companies, the London Midland and Scottish as well as the Great Western Railway. And down the road are the vans of Harding's the bakers, the heavier carts of the coal men, and the wagon's of Rudders and Payne's woodyard.

Then when the parading has finished, many of the men make their way to Calthorpe Park where their turn out is judged and prizes are given to the winners.

Sadly, the Maypole is no longer danced around in the street, and the customs of centuries have now fallen away. But at least there is still a parade of harness horses.

Girls and a couple of lads done up for the May Day Celebrations at Upper Highgate Street School, Highgate in 1929. Mildred Maddocks is circled standing on the left, and her pal Iris Reynolds is circled third from the left on the front row. Mildred lived in Emily Street by her granny and went to Upper Highgate Street until she was seven when she was moved to Chandos Road School. At eleven she was returned to Upper Highgate Street until she left school three years later.
(Thanks to Mildred Bradbury, born Maddocks).

BRUM BY THE SEA

He put down his Mail, twirled the ends of his moustache with his thumbs and forefingers, took out his old turnip from the pocket in his waistcoat, looked at it and then raised his eyes to check the time with the clock on the mantlepiece. Satisfied, he turned his head to the three children playing on the floor. "Right then," he started, and as he spoke they turned round to look at him, realising exactly what he was going to say. "Time for bed. Up the dancers!"

They knew better than to argue, but they tried a feeble "Oh dad..." knowing it would get them nowhere. Their mom put down her crocheting, smiling just a little. "Your dad's right. We've got a big day tomorrow, and you've got to get up early. Come on, up the wooden hill."

Off they trooped, with their dad's last words chasing them up the stairs. "And no larking about, you hear. Straight to sleep now." Excitedly they snuggled into bed, pulling their mom back, desperately trying to make her stay. "Where is Weston, mom?" "Why's it called Weston Super Mare, mom?" "What's the sea like mom?" "Can we make sandcastles, mom?"

On they went, repeating their questions until their patient mother finally lost her patience. "All right that's enough. If you don't go to asleep now we won't wake in time up to go to Weston tomorrow." They'd

Brummies and others on the beach in the early 1900s. Is it Weston? It looks it, going by the width of the beach and how far distant the sea is. Notice the donkeys, horse and cart, brollies and prams. (Thanks to Graham and Glenda Richards).

Joyce Greenhill (born Fox) as a baby with her family at the beach in Rhyl, 1929 or 1930. On the left of the sandcastle is Joyce's dad, William Henry Pearson, a policeman at Victoria Road Police Station, Aston; and behind her is her mom, Rose Amy Pearson (born Fox). Standing by Rose Amy are her sisters, Ethel and Ciss, and in front of them is Norman Brewin, Ciss's son. The family always went to Rhyl, taking with them the sister's disabled mother, Phoebe Emma Fox. (Thanks Joyce Greenhill).

swore to each other they wouldn't drop off and they'd repeated time and time again that they'd be up with the crack of dawn. But all their promises were broken as they drifted into a deep slumber, and they had to be shaken out of their dreams first thing.

"Wakey wakey, rise and shine you lot," said their dad. "You'd better get weaving, else we'll miss the train. Come on, get washed and let's get cracking." They helter-skeltered downstairs, where a bowl of hot water, carbolic soap and a towel was waiting for them. As quick as they could, they swilled their faces and flung themselves into their clothes, fretting in case they missed the train.

The old man winked at his wife. "I don't know whether we ought to stay at home, it's looking a bit black over Bill's mother's," he said. "I've got a feeling it's going to pelt down. Might as well stop here, eh love? No use going away if it'll be teeming." The reaction would be immediate. "No, dad. It'll be all right! I bet it's gonna be warm in Weston. Let's go, dad. Please!" Then they'd see the grin on his face and realise that he was having them on.

Every part of the day was such an adventure. Catching the tram into town, while the sun was still fighting to push back the dark of night, and listening to the banter of the driver. Traipsing up to the imposing entrance of Snow Hill Station, joining the scrum of folk going down the stairs, and then standing three and four deep on the platform, with their dad bestriding the family suitcase.

Finally the train arrived, brakes screeching, metal squealing, coal burning and steam billowing. What a sight! A great iron machine that sped along the tracks and with its grace and grandeur the eyes of each and every onlooker were dragged to it. Then there was a scramble to get on the train and the

real journey began. The kids' eyes were pressed to the window from the first minute to the last. Everything was so fresh and new. Green fields in which cows grazed, wooden hills, old churches, thatched cottages, winding lanes. The countryside was so different – it was wide and green and there were trees and birds everywhere.

"Do you know," their mom said. "I was married to your dad before I saw the sea for the first time, and that was a day trip to Blackpool. I couldn't believe it, it was so big, so huge. It seemed to go on for ever and ever. I just kept on staring at it. You don't know how lucky you are to have a proper holiday with a week away in a boarding house."

All day their dad kept telling them about the places they were passing through. "Look, this is Stratford, where Shakespeare was born. Bet you didn't know that. The greatest writer ever in the English language and he come from Warwickshire just like us. We're coming to Cheltenham now. This is where they have a big race meeting every year. Oh, and this is Gloucester. Do you know your grandad came from here and he was working on the boats when he was your age? From when he was eight he was grafting and collaring. I hope you appreciate how lucky you are."

Why was it that moms and dads always said that, again and again? Wasn't once enough? Then at last, came the words they were waiting for. "We're nearly there, now. This is Bristol. Next stop Weston."

Weston! Beaches, sand, making castles, seeing Punch and Judy, going for rides on a donkey, and wandering about seeing the sea. Walking along the front just having a mooch, trying to get a crafty glimpse of the postcards that dad laughed at and mom blushed at. That's what an English holiday was

all about. It didn't really matter if it rained because surely that was part of the holiday as well. Any road, I'm off to Weston. Have a good time and see you next week!

Huge crowds at Snow Hill Station, everyone waiting for a relief train to take them on holiday to the South Coast of England, 23 July 1949.

SIGHTS AND SOUNDS

SCHOOL OF HARD KNOCKS

"Sit up straight, shoulders back and let's see you quiet. Quickly now, else we'll be late for assembly and that would never do." Not a word of complaint, nor even a hint of a moan, because no-one dared to answer her back even if they thought of it - which few ever did.

Though she was a nice young teacher, tender to the little 'uns who blarted in the baby's class and kind to those who couldn't get things right, still she was a stickler for discipline. And one thing she wouldn't abide was a chatty class where the children didn't do as they were told - immediately. Right index finger across their tightly shut lips, the youngsters looked determinedly ahead, never thinking to shift their heads or even to glance at their pals with a sideways shift of their eyes. "That's good. Now fingers away from your mouths and let's see how fast you can fold you arms."

Scanning the room to see her instructions were carried out, she was soon satisfied. "Right, all stand and line up quickly at the door." No sooner said than done. She always had the most responsible kids at the desks in the front, knowing that when they set off for assembly she could trust them not to play

Miss Darby and her class, probably at St John's Deritend, about 1906. Miss Darby later taught at St Mary's C. of E. School, Aston Cross for nine years, followed by time at Vicarage Road, Council School, Aston. (Thanks to Mr and Mrs Darby).

A classroom scene at Denis Road School, Balsall Heath – sometime in the Edwardian age judging by the tops and collars of the lads. (Birmingham Library Services).

up by tipping and tapping each other. That left her free to hush the last youngsters out of class and to march alongside them.

The hall smelled of polished floor and chalk, as it was also used for teaching. It could be split into two by screens and had a blackboard at either end. Often kids on the one side could be heard chanting their times tables whilst from the other came the thump of feet doing PT. Directing her class almost to the front, the teacher made sure that they sat cross-legged in a smart row. In front stood the headmistress. The focal point of the whole school, she cut a striking figure. Her spotless blouse was buttoned up to almost under her chin, whilst her skirt flowed down to the floor and virtually covered her polished boots.

It seemed like she'd been at the school forever, and she'd even taught the moms and dads, aunts and uncles of some of the present scholars. Sharp-tongued, blunt and a bit of a tartar, she never suffered fools gladly. But for all that, one thing about her made the local parents respect and support her - the kids in her charge came first. That was her life.

One of the first generation of working-class kids to go to school full-time following the 1870 Education Act, she'd set her heart on becoming a teacher. By the time she was 11 she was looking after

a class of younger children, but when her dad died it seemed her hopes would be dashed. He'd had a good job and was happy for her to go on to become a pupil teacher but without his income it looked like she'd never make it.

She reckoned without her mom, who washed and scrubbed, maided and mended to help her daughter get on - a sacrifice she never forgot. Behind her harshness and forbidding looks was a woman who always remembered where she came from, who had a kind word for mothers with worry-lined brows and who strove daily to help her children get an education so that they would have a chance in life.

Each week, she'd reward a well-behaved or a hard-working pupil by letting them make her a dinner in the little room that served as a kitchen. Each week she made sure different kids had the honour of bringing the register. Each week she made sure she had a supply of rocks in her pockets to hand, off the cuff, to a youngster who caught her eye by doing something good.

She was a marvellous woman and the kids responded. They knew where they stood with her, for she never made fish of one and fowl of the other. She may have been swift to punish you but it was never out of malice, it was always when you deserved it, and she made sure to tell you the reasons for her actions. She did her best - like so many of the teachers of Old Brum.

Children in the classroom with their teacher at Upper Thomas Street School, 1922. Like St Michael's RC School in Digbeth, Upper Thomas Street was famed for the sporting success of its boys – one of whom was Johnny Prescott, the celebrated Brummie Boxer. (Thanks to Edith Price).

GATEWAY TO HELL:
THE WORKHOUSE

Workhouses. They were the Bastilles of England. Large and prison-like, their presence haunted the working class. They symbolised humiliation and indignity. They represented oppression and harshness. They stood for sorrow and suffering.

Throughout England, workhouse entrances were feared and hated. They were The Archways of Tears, through which the poor stepped unwillingly and unhappily. They knew what awaited them on the other side. Their independence would be torn from them; their freedom of action would be stolen from them. Even their humanity would be taken from them. An existence of misery and toil was to be their lot.

Many of the rich and powerful believed that the poor were workshy and feckless, that it was their own fault that they were struggling to survive. They asserted that the poor had to be forced to work, and they declared that poverty was a crime to be punished. For them, the workhouse was a place of

The archway of tears, the entrance to the old workhouse in Western Road. (Thanks to City Hospital)

Galleries at the workhouse in Winson Green., 24 February 1958. The staff would parade along these to keep an eye on the poor folk below who had no choice but to go into the 'house' and to scrub the floors, break stones and do other arduous tasks for their keep.

correction. It was there to dissuade the poor from asking for relief.

The Victorian age was a time when the state ignored the plight of the ill, the disabled, the old, the unemployed and the low-paid. These people looked to their families and neighbours for help, but still some had to seek assistance from charities, or the Guardians of the Poor. These men levied a rate on property-owners in their district, and out of it they granted relief to those who they thought were deserving.

Will Thorne's mother was one of those who had no choice but to go "on the parish." She lived in Farm Street, Hockley, and in the 1850s she was left a widow with seven children. She was granted four loaves and four shillings a week for her family to live on. The bread was "about as bad as it could be," and the seven-year-old Thorne had to walk two miles to fetch it.

But if someone applied to the parish too often, they were told that they had to go into "the house." It mattered not if there was no work available, it mattered not if they were upstanding and decent, it mattered not if they were victims of circumstances beyond their control.

What a dreadful scene it was as a family gathered despairingly outside the Archway of Tears in Western Road, Winson Green! The little 'uns would be blarting and clinging to their mom's frock and the look of grief in their mom's face was enough to break the hearts of passers-by. The big 'uns were silent and unmoving - except for the tears which fell from eyes heavy with anguish. And there stood the old man, desolate and shattered by the step he was about to take.

He'd knock on the door, reluctantly and weakly - but his knock would be heard. The gate opened, and the family trudged forward disconsolately. A guard would take them across a courtyard into a building. Here the mother and the girls were pulled away from the man and boys, and put into a room. They were stripped and bathed, then given a uniform. Then they would be marched across another

courtyard into the workhouse proper. The father drew his sons to him, and the mother wrapped her arms around her girls, sending despairing looks at her chap. But he could do nothing.

At the end of the long corridor there was a "T-junction." A female warder grabbed the mother's hand and dragged her roughly and unwillingly to the left, while a male warder pushed the father and sons into another corridor on the right.

But that wasn't the end of the humiliation. The boys would be tugged from their father; the girls grasped away from their mother. The family was broken up.

Husbands and wives were allowed to meet just once a week - and then only under supervision to prevent them from making love and so bringing into the world more children. And all of them had to work to pay for their food and their bed. The father toiled at breaking stones or picking oakum. The mother laboured in a laundry and the children scrubbed the floors clean. They were beaten mercilessly if they didn't do their tasks as they were told.

The only way to escape from the workhouse was to show that you could support yourself outside. Perhaps younger people could do that, but the old had no chance.

Once they passed through the Archway of Tears, they were condemned to a life sentence. When they died, they were subjected to the greatest indignity of all - a burial in a pauper's grave. But if no stone marks their living, then we today should keep their memories alive. We should never forget the poor of Old Brum who had to go into the workhouse.

Interior shot of workhouse building in Winson Green. Much of the place was knocked down in the 1950s, although parts were turned Summerfield Hospital for old Folks. The stigma of the workhouse was so great, though, that many elderly people refused to go into Summerfield. One good did come out of the vile workhouse system, for it had to develop infirmaries, one of which later became Dudley Road Hospital, now known as City Hospital. (Thanks to City Hospital)

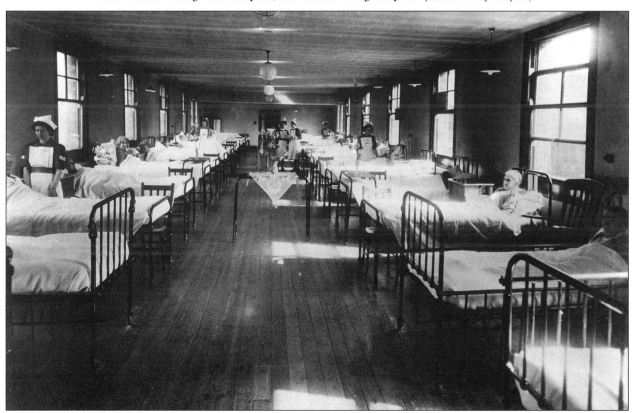

WHAT A WASTE:
THE RAILWAY STATIONS OF BRUM

What a roof! It was a huge archway of glass and corrugated iron - wide, deep and staggering to the onlooker. Parts of the great roof were shrouded in clouds of smoke which wafted up from the factories on the banks of the Rea. Other portions were covered by billows of steam, which were belched out by the engines below. But nothing could hide the breathtaking size and scope of the roof. It was the largest in the world - and it covered Birmingham's New Street Station.

The measurements of the roof were awe-inspiring. It was 1,080 feet long, and spanned 212 feet. And it rested on 45 massive pillars. These were spread out on either side of the station, and each weighed over 5.5 tons. The weight of the roof was even more awesome. It was made up of 120,000 feet of glass and 100,000 feet of iron sheeting. Bearing down on the pillars was the colossal weight of 2,415 tons!

Despite its vastness, the roof was not ungainly. Nor was it cumbersome. To onlookers who gazed at it in admiration, it appeared to be light and graceful. It was a wonderful building, and one of the world's greatest engineering achievements. Yet it was knocked down, its glass shattered, ironwork

New Street Station in the early 1900s with Queen's Drive running through the middle of the photo and St Martin's Church spire in the background. (Thanks to Mr T. Nichols).

The Famous booking hall of Snow Hill Station and its magnificent clock, probably just after its completion in 1912.

broken and pillars smashed. It was the finest railway station in the world. Yet it was laid waste. Magnificent staircases which led to the platforms were destroyed. A beautiful refreshment room was demolished. This symbol of Victorian ingenuity and industry was obliterated. So, too, was Snow Hill Station, the terminal for the Great Western Railway. Red bricks, glass roof, stone cornices and moulded corbels - all shattered and ruined.

Buildings of grandeur and style were swept away, to be replaced by functional and modern structures. At the same time, the locomotives which used the stations were altered. Steam and coal were overwhelmed by diesel power. Trains which had combined purpose with romance were replaced by machines that did a job but had less glamour.

Across Birmingham, the sounds of the railways changed. And not just in the stations and on the lines, but in the goods yards too. In Tyseley and Saltley, in Vauxhall and Brookfields, in Bordesley and Hockley, generations of Brummies had grown up used to the clashing of buffers, the clinging of couplings, the hooting of horns and the hissing of steam. These noises were part of daily life. No-one really noticed them - until the day they stopped. Then their silence roared. It shouted out that there was a new railway system. It exclaimed that the age of steam was dead. It declared that there were less jobs.

Where are the tens of thousands of men who drove the trains, who stoked them full with coal, who signalled them on their way, who cleaned them and who maintained them? Where are the porters, the clerks, the electricians and the carters? And where are all the horses that were stabled in Lawley Street and elsewhere? Horses that helped to provide food for hundreds of Brummie kids.

There they'd be, little figures in short trousers and ganseys traipsing behind the railway wagons, bucket and shovel in hand, waiting patiently until the horses dropped their manure. Then it was scooped up and off raced the kids - to a 'posh' house with a garden, whose owners wanted to help their rhubarb grow. And with the ha'penny earned they could run to an eating house and buy a piece of bread dipped in the fat of roasting meat.

So much has gone. But some symbols of Old Brum's railways remain. Have a mooch down New Canal Street to the corner of Curzon Street, and look up at the station opposite. Built in 1838, it's three stories high and is guarded by four massive columns at the front and two at the back. Then saunter along to Lawley Street and stare at the Birmingham Viaduct, just as did one visitor to Brum in 1851. He was so impressed by the 28 arches he saw that he cried out "it was a stupendous work challenging comparison with almost any ancient or modern art!"

Just behind it, crossing over to Landor Street, lies another striking blue-brick viaduct - part of the old London and Midland Railway Line. And there are more of these magnificent monuments to engineering endeavour. There's the viaduct which runs south east from Moor Street Station, gaining height and stature as it travels across the Rea towards Camp Hill. Looping off the line is a viaduct which has never been used. Made up of 58 arches, it covers 1,100 yards and was intended to go from Bordesley to Curzon Street. It never reached its destination - yet it dominates the landscape, overshadowing the nearby factories and works, a reminder of the workers who grafted to forge the landscape of Old Brum.

Sorting out the bales at Lawley Street Goods Station, 1 November 1945.

CHAPEL DAYS TO CHERISH

They'd had to scrat for everything they'd got. Each week they'd dipped into their pockets and put on the plate as much as they could - mostly thruppenny bits and tanners, but occasionally a bob or two. Each week they'd stood on street corners preaching the Gospel, with a flat cap on the floor to hold the farthings and ha'pennies flung down by sympathetic listeners. Each week they'd gone out selling religious tracts for whatever they could get, sometimes returning home empty-handed and despondent. And each week they'd pulled together, sung together and worshipped together for the glory of God.

Often they'd thought they'd never realise their ambition of having their own chapel. The task seemed too hard, the road too long. But when they were at their lowest ebb something always seemed to come up - as if God was telling them not to pack it in. Once they'd got so down in their spirits that

Harvest Festival at Mr Wilson's Chapel, Theodore Street, 1920s. The chapel was just a room over some stables which was reached by wooden stairs. Mr Wilson himself had a furniture business locally and on Sundays would meet each of the children coming to his mission with a little bag of jelly. (Thanks to Edith Davis whose Aunt Elise used to play the piano for the hymn singing at the mission).

Children singing at Ladypool Road Congregational Chapel, perhaps late 1930s. In 1900 the Sparkbrook Gospel Mission was founded, meeting in a corrugated iron building. Five years later and with help from Moseley Road Congregational Church a site was bought on the Ladypool Road for the building of a proper chapel. It was opened for worship on 6 May 1908 and was dedicated by Dr J. H. Jowett, minister of Carr's Lane Church. During the Second World War the chapel was hit by incendiaries and the roof was burnt off. A new one was installed by 1950 and the chapel continues with its mission. (Thanks to Ladypool Road Congregational Church).

they'd almost decided to go and join an older and better established chapel and out of the blue they'd been given some money by the relatives of a kindly old lady who'd passed away.

With enough cash to buy a bit of land they traipsed the footpaths looking for a site. They found it, squeezed between a factory and a terrace of houses and hemmed in by a railway line at the rear and a back street at the front. It worn't much to outsiders, but to them it was everything and now they could plan properly for building their own place of worship. Reinvigorated, once again they dedicated themselves to raising the funds they needed to realise their hopes.

At last they managed to save up enough money to buy some wood and to put up a hut for themselves. They would have preferred to have made their tabernacle with sheets of corrugated iron, but they couldn't stretch to that expense. Still, they were chuffed to bits when it was finished.

It may not have had any architectural merit but it meant as much to them as any of the great churches and chapels elsewhere in Brum.

There was just one door and a couple of little windows on either side. Within the furnishings were simple - a table for the preacher, a few rough benches and a cupboard. The mostly bare walls were decorated only by the odd stricture like "The Lord is My Shepherd" and "Blessed is He who comes in the name of the Lord." That was it, but it was better than the hall they used to hire from the local school and which never belonged to them. And it was certainly better than where they'd first met years back, in a tiny room in and old cottage which was home to one of their fellows.

Having their own place meant that they had a proper base and they could start doing more for the local people as well as for themselves. They hung up notices about their services, they set up a Sunday School, they arranged Bible Classes for Young Men, and they even started a cycling club. Most Sundays its members set off from the chapel after the morning service, always returning in time for prayers in the early evening. With so much going on, there was little doubt that the chapel was a success.

There were places like this dotted throughout Old Brum. In Bartley Green the Primitive Methodists gathered in the little Adams Hill Ebenezer Chapel, which had room for only a score or so people. In Selly Oak and Bournbrook, the Brethren met first in someone's home then in a Gospel Tent and last in a wooden chapel in Tiverton Road, which has since been rebuilt in brick. Meanwhile in Victoria Road, Handsworth, the local Baptists worshipped in an iron-sheeted building which held 200 folk and which cost £240 when it was erected in 1885. And in Buck Street, the Wesleyans of the Sea Horse Hall made do with a building which once had been a pub.

Of course, there were plenty of bigger and grander chapels - like the magnificent Central Hall in Corporation Street. Resplendent in its terracotta facing and eye-catching because of the illuminated cross in its tower, it could take in 2,000 people. A similar number used to pack into the Greek-style Mount Zion Chapel in Graham Street to hark at the words of the celebrated preacher George Dawson. And hundreds followed him in 1846 when he moved to the splendid Church of the Saviour in Edward Street - later the

Lyric Picture House.

But it didn't really matter what size the chapel was, or what it was made of. The most important thing was to meet and to praise God. It wasn't materials which made the chapels of Old Brum - it was the people. Have a happy and holy Easter.

The Church of Christ in Great Francis Street, Bloomsbury late 1950s. The chapel was in use by 1885, although there had been a congregation locally from 1873. It had room for 120 worshippers and by 1956 had a membership of 54. (Thanks to Johnny Landon).

LOTS IN STORE:
GREY'S

It was the busiest shopping thorough-fare in Birmingham. Each day, bar Sunday when the pigeons took over, Bull Street was packed with folk drawn to the well-known retailers. There was Southall the chemist, Harris the dyer, Page and Grundy the ladies costumier and many more - all vying for attention with big drapery stores such as Lewis's, Newberry's and Rackham's. It was unusual for anyone to halt for long in that vibrant street – even browsers in shop windows were swayed by the crowds. But one day in 1891 a man did stand still amidst the hurry - yet though he didn't move he wasn't doing nothing. His mind was working ten to the dozen.

Facing Flint's the silk mercer and supplier of linen at number 66, he rapidly reckoned up the people passing by as swiftly he weighed up the potential appeal of the premises. Eventually, his mind was made up. He'd buy the shop. It was in a cracking position, just before Temple Row, and he knew he could make it attractive.

It was a big step. He'd have to pack up his job as a buyer of drapery for Lewis's and set up on his own. Neither conceited nor arrogant, still he was self-confident in his own skills and was certain he'd

Edna Craddock, sitting at the front, and other members of Grey's Tennis Club at Grove Lane, Handsworth, 1928 or 1929. On the back row are Frank Ford, the two Misses Street, Ernest Slater, Mable Titmus and Ivy Street. (Thanks to Edna Craddock).

Grey's store in Steelhouse Lane, just down from the corner with Bull Street, 1959.

make a good job of it. After all, he was successful in his job, he knew how to buy well and he believed that he had the attributes to be a good seller and a clever businessman. Soon after Edward Greey opened his fancy goods shop, dropping the one 'e' from his name so that it would be more readily recognised and easier for trading purposes. Immediately, he set out his stall. He would always provide goods at value for money and he would attract a loyal clientele, through quality products at keen prices, and personal service.

Edward Greey's approach pulled in the customers and within a few years he bought the premises next door - and more. By 1914 he owned numbers 65, 66, 66a, 67, 69, 70, 71 and 72 - and not long after he took over number 68. Knocking down the dividing walls between his properties and converting the bedrooms on the second floors, he added more departments.

For all the growth, Grey's was intimate and chatty - more like a cosy village shop than a big city department store. That feeling remained as strong after the old buildings were knocked down and Grey's became one huge building, dominating the west side of Bull Street and visible all the way down Colmore Row. Greeted by smart and proud commissionaires, shoppers came into the ground floor for hosiery and wool. Above were floors devoted to the sale of ladies underwear; ladieswear; and furniture, carpets and net. Then on the fifth floor was a restaurant and offices, over which were storerooms, staff canteens and curtain making rooms.

The founder of the business died in 1925, soon after his grand new establishment was opened. He was succeeded by his three sons who clung fast to their father's trading principles. They were supported

by loyal and keen workers who were noted for their attachment to Grey's. In fact in 1938, 33 employees had been with the family since before 1914 - and, of these, seven had started before 1900. One of them, Mr S. Cooke, was now warehouse manager after beginning in 1896 as a clerk.

Customers liked that personal touch of being served by someone who knew them and they were also attracted by the talented musicians who played Palm Court-type melodies at Grey's restaurant - men like Ernest Freedman the pianist, Vernon Adcock the drummer, Charles Warren the violinist and Raymond Marchant the cellist.

The appeal of Grey's of Bull Street was carried over into the new stores opened by the company in Steelhouse Lane, Dudley, Walsall, Stourbridge, Rugby and Leamington. With its motto 'Grey's Serve You Right' the firm continued to expand after 1945 until it was taken over by Debenham's. The new owners dropped the name Grey's and something was lost from Brum. Then in 1983 the business was closed, and the building knocked down. Grey's may be gone but many of us remember it affectionately as Birmingham's Own Store.

Edna Gate-Hunter, known as 'Gate', saying goodbye to her pals at Grey's, 15 October 1982. Edna worked at the store for 45 years, starting as a sales assistant in the wool department for ten shillings a week. The best wool sold at 6d an ounce but the most popular was a penny three farthings.

AS BRUM SLEPT:
THE MARKETS

The streets were empty - bar some bits of paper scuffing about in the light breeze. The buildings were sombre, except for an odd window shown up by the shimmering light of a candle. The night air itself was still - save for the occasional bobowler flitting about . Even the starlings in the Minories were silent. It seemed as if the whole world slumbered. The whole world, that is, apart from the Birmingham Markets.

While most other people rested, the trading folk of Brum were hard a collar. Since the early hours of the morning farmers, merchants, shopkeepers and hawkers had been making their way towards one of the greatest wholesale markets in the land - Smithfield. With carts, wagons and barrows they came through a clutch of tight streets whose names were steeped in Brum's history. Some favoured Spiceal Street, running alongside St Martin's and then shooting down into Jamaica Row. Others moved through St Martin's Lane or else up Smithfield Street and Moat Lane. Many made their way along Sherlock Street and Bradford Street. And still more dragged themselves laboriously towards perhaps the most bustling place of all - the junction of Dean Street.

A view of Smithfield Market in the early 1900s.

A busy morning at Francis Nicholls Ltd in Smithfield Market, April 1936

By 5 o'clock in the morning this handful of little lanes was heaving with people and horses, so much so that there was many an accident at the spot where they flowed one into the other. Amidst the hurry scurry, blokes with hand carts bobbed and weaved skilfully through the long lines of slow-moving traffic, their balance and speed made more extraordinary by the stacks of fruit and vegetables piled in front of them. Once they'd got shut of their loads then back towards Smithfield they'd scoot, ready to stock up again and once more dart about their business.

Outside the great building, the pavements were packed with produce of every kind brought in by traders who couldn't find room within - not a bad pitch in the summer when the skies were clear but lousy in the winter when it was parky and wet.

But it was the scene inside the red brick walls of Smithfield which was the most fascinating of all. As dawn broke, light thrust itself through the big doors throwing everything into vivid relief. Tall, cast pillars stretched from the floor to the ceiling and piles of crates went up and up, so high that without a shadow of a doubt it looked as if they'd topple. But they didn't, put up as they were by fellers who knew their game inside out.

Here and there oblongish signs hung down from the roof, proclaiming the name of a wholesaler. Many of them were long-established and well-known - like Francis Nicholls, Vickerstaffs, Arthur Edmonds, Davis and Randle, George Haines and others. Beneath each label were gathered buyers and sellers, each one seeking to do the best deal that was possible and ready to strike it with a shake of the

hand and a word given. It was a confusing but captivating sight. There seemed no order yet every person knew what he was doing and got on with it.

But it wasn't only the eyes that were overwhelmed by Smithfield. So too, was every other sense. The smells of cabbages, caulis, swedes and turnips pushed for attention against those of pears, oranges, grapes and plums. Now and then someone would bite into a tomato or an apple to taste it for its freshness and appeal. Regularly potatoes were scratched so that their skins were broken and they could be examined for their moistness and whiteness, while other expert hands felt bananas which had come from ripening vaults nearby.

Then there was the noise. What a cacophony of cries and calls rent the air!

Men shouted for notice, roared "Mind out the road!,' bellowed for help and yelled what they'd got. And in the background was the rumble of motors, the whinnying of horses and the clatter of the iron-shod wheels of the barrows on the cobblestones.

It had been like that since the late 1800s when the pig and cattle market was moved to Montague Street and Smithfield was given over fully to the sale of fruit and vegetables. It stayed like that until the mid 1970s when the new market complex was opened and the red bricks of Smithfield were swept away. Still, if the building has gone, at least the wholesalers and market traders remain as a vital and essential link with Old Brum.

Mr A. F. Davis with the trilby, President of the Birmingham Wholesale Fruit and Potato Association, chatting with traders and wholesalers about the traffic hazards at the junction of Dean Street, Upper Dean Street and Gloucester Street, 15 July 1962.

CITY OF A THOUSAND TRADES

OTTO THE GERMAN
GOT BSA CYCLING

Things were looking rough for the BSA, the world famous gun-making firm in Small Heath. The government was always quick to call on the Brummie workers when weapons were needed urgently for our troops – but when peace came it was the same old story. What little orders there were for arms went to the Royal Ordnance factories in London. The Brummagem grafters were left to scrat and scrape as best they could, and that's what they had to do in the winter of 1878.

There worn't no doubt, it was a bad 'un. There was no collar, it was parky and bellies were empty. Things didn't pick up much in the following 18 months and it seemed as if the BSA's gaffers would have to chuck it. Then out of the blue, something turned up. A German bloke call F.C. Otto popped into the factory just on the off-chance – and he fetched with him the strangest looking contraption. It had two

The spectacular arch put up by the cycle trade in New Street in July 1909. You can just see the Town Hall in the background. Magnificent arches were also put up by the city's firemen, Water Department and others – all to celebrate the visit of King Edward VII and Queen Alexendra to open The University of Birmingham at Edgbaston. This photo was taken by Mrs D. Waites' father-in-law. He was a keen amateur photographer and worked at the BSA. (Thanks to Mrs D. Waite).

The bicycle shop of O. W. Hopkins in Great Lister Street, Duddeston, about 1928. His son Jack Hopkins is with him on the photo and for many years Jack has run a well-known bicycle business on Robin Hood in Hall Green. (Thanks to Jack Hopkins)

large wheels which were connected by a horizontal tube, from which rose a saddle and below which were two pedals. It was a bicycle and Herr Otto showed it off to the BSA's directors on their boardroom table before riding off down the twisty stairs! Knocked back a bit but quite impressed by his swank, the gaffers took a chance. They might as well have a go at manufacturing bikes. After all, what could they lose?

Over the next couple of years the BSA turned out almost a thousand machines to Otto's specifications and they also started to send out their own cycles and tricycles. Still it wasn't enough to really make a difference to the company's fortunes and then a few of the workers themselves had an idea. Why not produce a "safety" bicycle, something smaller and easier to move along than the cumbersome penny-farthings which were so common?

With materials cadged from this shop and that department and with scrap metal salvaged from the tip, they set to. They had no drawings other than sketches scratched on to the factory walls and they had few tools bar their Brummagem hands. And what hands they were! When they'd finished those Small Heath lads made the world's first rear-driven bicycle and a saddle far enough back that the riders couldn't come a purler over the handlebars.

The BSA was set on its way to becoming an internationally renowned maker of bicycles, but it wasn't the only firm pushed into seeking a new product by hard times. The Wolseley Sheep Shearing Company and Kynoch's the ammunition manufacturer were also drawn into the cycle trade by its

popularity at a time when their main businesses were struggling. So too were a number of sewing machine companies.

Faced with a drop in demand for their products, Thomas and James Crompton, Buckingham and Adams and William Andrews all shifted their machinery into making bicycles. In fact, the works manager of Andrews soon moved on to start up his own bike-producing business. His name was Harry James and by the inter-war years his factory in Tomey Road, Greet was noted across the five continents.

There were plenty of other well-known bicycle firms in Brum, including the New Hudson of Garrison Lane, and just across the border in Smethwick was the major business of J.A. Phillips. But there was no doubt as to which was the biggest bike works in the world. That title was held proudly by Hercules of Rocky Lane, Aston. Its name was seen and admired wherever cycles were ridden – from the United Kingdom to North Africa and from South America to the Indian subcontinent. Indeed, by the middle of the 1930s the company had over 4,000 workers producing more than 750,000 machines each year.

In both world wars the bicycle makers of Brum did their duty – sending out not only military bikes but also a multitude of other war goods. Yet in the years after 1945 these manufacturers faced difficult

times. Gradually they were swallowed up by bigger concerns. Soon their workers were laid off, their gates were chained together and their premises were closed down. New Hudson, the James, the Hercules – all are gone. Still two Brummie firms continue the tradition of bicycle production in Birmingham. Kirk and Merefield in Bradford Street and Dawes Cycles of Tyseley both hold fast proudly to the bike-making skills of Old Brum.

Women on the production line in a Birmingham bicycle factory, 1950s.

BRUM HAD THE WRITE STUFF:
PEN MAKING

Brum in the 1800s was a town where metal sang. In every street and every yard a multitude of smiths collared with hammers and tongs, stamps and presses, drawbenches and lathes. As they clanged and clashed, they formed the goods which were desired across the world. They took iron and crafted bedsteads, they grasped brass and fashioned light fittings, they clutched gold and created jewellery. They gripped copper and struck coins. Whatever the metal, the folk of Brum could work it and shape it into a thing of beauty.

A skilful people, they were also resourceful, clever and ingenious. Just as their hands were deft so too their minds were sharp. Continually they searched to find quicker and better ways to make their wares and increasingly they sought to discover a new manufacture which would have a great impact.

Visit of the Prince of Wales to the Victoria Works of Joseph Gillott in Victoria Street, Hockley, The Graphic, 7 November 1874.

A scene from Gillott's, 1919.

The inventiveness of Brummies was renowned and it is little wonder that the city was alluring to imaginative and adroit people from far and wide. It was to Brummagem that came two great Scots - James Watt to develop his steam engine and William Murdock to realise his dream of lighting the gas given off by burning coal. And to Brum came also the Worcestershire lad John Baskerville with his ambition to make a form of type unsurpassed in the world, and the American Dr William Church with his idea of chilling castings.

There were many more – amongst them those who opened up the art of writing to millions of ordinary men and women. For it was here in Brummagem that writing was democratised. Just think of it. Before the steel pen nib came along how did someone write? They had to have a reed or a goose quill - both of which were expensive to buy and difficult to use.

But then came along a group of blokes who turned out tens of millions of steel pen nibs each year, cheap and easy to handle. Among them was Josiah Mason, a poor Kidderminster lad who traipsed to Brum when there was a depression in the carpet industry. Then there was Joseph Gillott who tramped to Birmingham when there was a downturn in the steel trade of Sheffield. And there were also a number of Brummies born and bred, like a chap called Brandauer, John Heath and William Mitchell, whose sister married Gillott.

In the late 1820s these men all seemed to be inspired, individually and collectively. They began to make steel pen nibs with screw presses, pushing out the shape of a nib from a strip of metal. At first the process was slow and awkward but these men kept on devising new ways of making it faster and dextrous.

Their success was spectacular. By the 1870s they and other local firms were manufacturing upwards of 20 million pens each week! And at such a low cost, for they were made for as little as three ha'pence a gross, compared to five bob for 144 in the 1830s.

The outstanding popularity of these pens meant regular work for thousands of Brummies. Mason made his pens for a man called James Perry, and at his factory in Lancaster Street there were over a 1,000 employees, most of whom were women. These people rolled the steel bought from Sheffield, they cut out the blanks and pierced them; slit, raised and shaped them; and stamped, scoured and ground them until they were ready for sale.

Marked with the words 'Made in Birmingham' such pens went out to Britain and Ireland, across Western Europe and throughout North America. Their importance was immense in bringing literacy to the widest number of people, and their influence was recognised by Elihu Burritt, the American Consul in Birmingham. In 1868 he visited Gillott's factory, the Victoria Works in Graham Street which dominated the brow of New Hall Hill. The American was awestruck by the activity, energy and adeptness which he saw there. He exclaimed that Gillott was a 'pioneer of civilisation' because in 'ten thousand school-houses scattered over the American continent between the two oceans; a million children used the Brummagem entrepeneur's pens.

Burritt finished off by saying that Gillott's was "the great lion of Birmingham manufacturers to Americans visiting the town". Such praise was not exceptional. Brummagem's pens were the finest and the best. It's little surprise that Old Brum was celebrated as the 'pen shop of the world'.

Viewing the pens, 1950s.

THIRST FOR SUCCESS:
BREWERIES

You name it, we made it - from pins to brass bedsteads, from coins to bicycles, from paraffin lamps to motor cars. From jewellery to railway carriages, from buttons to motorbikes, and from pen nibs to steam engines, we made it. Throughout the world, Brum's workers were famed for their craft in fashioning metal into goods of beauty and usefulness. Brass, gold, silver, copper, steel and nickel - all were shaped by the press, the stamp, the drawbench and the lathe.

But the skills of Brummies were not restricted to the working of metal. Theirs was the city of a thousand trades and they themselves could turn their hands to a multitude of tasks. The manufacture of glass and rubber? No problem. The production of gas and electricity? No problem. Old Brum could take on any task. From the making of chocolate and custard to the brewing of vinegar and beer, Birmingham had the skills - and the thirst for success.

The 'Bank Tavern' on the corner of New John Street West and Great Russell Street, Summer Lane neighbourhood, early 1900s. The pub is advertising Holder's Ales, one of the many breweries in Brum at that time, which was based in Nova Scotia Street. Sir John Holder owned and laid out the area of Sir John's Road, Selly Park. His brewery was taken over by M. and B. in 1919.
(Thanks to Don Davis).

Davenport's horse-drawn carts lined up and laden with bottles of beer, probably 1920s – is it Bath Row that they're in?

In the middle of the 1800s, there were hundreds of brewers in Brum. Nearly every pub and beer house had its copper and brew'us. Some of these premises are with us still like the 'Bellefield' in Winson Green, the 'Wellington' in Gooch Street and The 'Waggon and Horses' in Adderley Street. But many are gone - just as the smaller makers of beer have disappeared, too.

From the 1880s, they were swallowed up by common brewers like William Butler of 'The Crown' on Broad Street, who began by brewing for himself, but then started to sell the surplus to other publicans. His next move was to buy other licensed premises as outlets for his product, and then in 1898 he became a partner with Henry Mitchell of Smethwick. But Mitchell's and Butler's wasn't the biggest firm in the trade. That position was held by Holt's

This company developed from the brewing and malting operations of the Fulford's which went back as far as 1819. Originally it was based in Hospital Street, and its product was proclaimed as "Birmingham's best beer". Nearby was Kendrick's of Brearley Street, which closed down in the late 1920s. Not too far away, Brewery Street took its name from the Britannia Brewery which once stood there.

The adjacent district of Aston boasted abundant water supplies which were ideal for making beer - and many of Brum's breweries were to be found here, between the Hockley Brook and the River Rea. On Aston Cross rose up the imposing premises of Ansells. The firm's symbol was a triple 'A' arranged in a triangle and set in a circle, around which were the words "Ansells Aston Ales". And up the hill in Holt Street, off Tower Road, was the Vulcan Brewery of Alfred Homer who brewed "noted mild and bitter ales".

Then along the Aston Road itself was the Lion Brewery of W T Rushton who begged "to call special attention to the Trade to the quality of his Ales which are noted for their purity and excellence". Down the Lichfield Road was the Aston Model Brewery of Frederick Smith whose beer "is so enjoyable" and further up in Queens Road was situated Atkinson's brewery, whose slogan was "Held up as the best".

But brewers weren't absent from the rest of Brum. There were so many more. There was Guy's of Newdegate Street in Vauxhall, Holder's of Nova Scotia Street, Dare's of Belgrave Road and Davenport's of Bath Row. Following a spate of take-overs, Ansells and Davenport's were the last two firms remaining in the city by the late 1970s. Sadly, like all the other breweries of Old Brum, these two have also closed down. The fine water of Birmingham goes to waste and all the talents of brewing are neglected and forgotten - except at Aston Manor Brewery in Thimblemill Lane. Let's hope this firm continues the tradition of brewing in Brum. Cheers!

Violet Harding (later Wood) on the roof of Guy's Brewery in Newdegate Street, Vauxhall. Violet was born and raised nearby and started at Guy's as a very young girl. Like Davenport's, Guy's was well known for its bottled beer and delivery service.
(Thanks to Rita Penrice).

HARDEST WORKERS IN BRUM:
MOMS

It's well before the sun has broken through the morning darkness, and the lamp-lighter has yet to dowt the gas lights and start knocking up his customers from their slumbers. The machines in the local factories are motionless and silent, and even the deliverymen have not begun to clatter across the cobble-stoned streets. Everywhere is hushed, everyone seems to be asleep - all except for a shadowy figure heading across the yard to the brew'us.

A hard-wearing urden pinny is fastened across her midriff, she's carrying a bucket and she lights her way with a guttering candle. She steps into the dilapidated wash-house, feeling the cold as the wind blows through the glassless windows and the doorway which lacks a door. In front of her lies the big sink set in red bricks. She pulls the bucket up, places it beneath the tap, fills it with water and then empties it in the copper.

She looks around expectantly, and then she hears the sound she wants - the clumping of Daily Mail boots. Within seconds she's joined by the big 'un, the little mother of the family, who's got two pennyworth of slack in another bucket. As her mom carries on loading the water, the child hurriedly places the fuel beneath the boiler and lights it. Then she cops hold of a penny packet of Lively Polly and sprinkles it into the warming water.

A woman standing tired-looking outside the brew'us back of 14, Florence Street off Holloway head, March 1933. Notice the woman and the child actually in the brew'us and the mangle under the lean-to. (Thanks to Sylvia Leigh).

Banging the mats clean, probably late 1940s.

The wearisome labour goes on, as bucketful follows bucketful. And when the water's bubbling it's taken back out and poured into a wooden maiding tub - once used for carrying beer, now an essential washday tool. That's the signal for more hard collar. The older woman takes up her dolly, the wooden punch she uses to pound the clothes clean, and she gets cracking - 'cus there's no time to stop.

As she begins to pump and beat, her daughter traipses back across the yard which is now coming alive. People are tramping to the shared lavatories, pushing the sleep from their eyes with their knuckles, whilst others are beginning to set off for work.

The girl nods hello to other young wenches who are about their tasks, and when she's in her house she shakes the little 'uns awake and gets the porridge warmed up for them. Then she doles out their chores. The babbies have got to tidy up, while the two older lads've got to fetch a basket carriage, chase up to the vicar's house, get the choir's surplices and bring 'em to their mom. And they know that after school they'll have to go back with them - washed, starched and ironed.

By now their mother's well into her stride. She's finished maiding, and she's set to scrub and swill the clothes - before boiling them once again in clean water. But that's not the end of it. She's got to dip the whites in to a bucket of Reckitt's Blue to try and freshen clothes that are fading, and then she has to put shirts and collars into a bucket of starch.

When that's all done, it's time to squeeze out the water from the sodden clothes. She puts the washing in a bowl, and wearily carries it over to the mangle which stands beneath the window of her house. It's dinner-time already, and it's lucky that she put the stewpot on as soon as she got up. The

kids get stuck into their grub, helping themselves, and then they rush outside with a cup of tea for her, ready to give her a hand at the mangling. How many Brummie wenches, how many Brummie kids have had their fingers injured badly when they got them caught up in the motions of the mangle?

If it's fine, she can peg the clobber out on the line, but if it's wet, she's got no option - she'll have to hang the washing on lines stretched out across the one downstairs room of her tiny back-to-back. She knows the old man and the kids can't a-bare the heavy, damp smell which pervades the whole house. But it's got to be done. She's got to dry her own clothes and the surplices so she can get cracking on the ironing.

And that's a day's graft in itself, with the old flat iron which had to be heated up on the oven before it could be used. And suddenly, the day's drawing to a close.

School's over the lads are ready to fetch back the surplices - she's still got so much more to do. She gets stuck in, not leaving the brew'us till late at night.

Then, last of all, she carries buckets of water to the top of the stairs, chucking them down so that she can scrub the wood clean. The moms of Old Brum. They worked all their lives.

Charles Willey going back to the yard in Anderton Street in which he grew up, 4 February 1965. Look at the woman sweeping the yard and the mop and bucket outside the other woman's house.

CELEBRATION OF INDUSTRY:
MUSEUM OF SCIENCE AND INDUSTRY

Although it was now empty and forlorn, once Elkington's Electro-Plate factory in Newhall Street, Hockley, had been one of the most celebrated factories in the world. From every corner of the globe it had drawn in onlookers eager to see how silver and gold were fused onto base metal and then raised and fashioned into works of art. In 1868 an American called Elihu Burritt captured the amazement of these admiring visitors. He exclaimed that Elkington's 1,000 workers represented "as much highly-trained genius and skill as was ever brought together under the same roofage".

Yet within 100 years the famed business had been taken over and its renowned works were closed. Silent and solemn, it seemed that no longer did they have a purpose. Then George Cadbury had a cracking idea. Why shouldn't Birmingham have a museum filled with machines and matters to do with science and industry? After all, few other towns or cities could claim as vital a role in the making of the modern world.

Old George set about making things happen. Through his chairmanship of the Common Good Trust the money was provided to buy one of James Watt's rotative engines as well as an engine made by Richard

The entrance to the Museum of Science and Industry in Newhall Street, 5 August 1952. It still shows the Elkington's crest and proclaims 'Electro Plate works'.

A tilt hammer for forging and supposedly about 200 years old, presented to the Museum of Science and Industry by A. and F. Parkes of Dartmouth Street, manufacturers of garden and edge tools and agricultural implements, 12 November 1952.

Trevethick, a pioneer of steam locomotion. Then George paid for a beam engine to be brought from Stourbridge to Bournville where it was put into working order. Last he purchased a collection of copies of drawings by the Italian genius Leonardo da Vinci.

Cadbury's enthusiasm was matched by that of the city council. Even before the Second World War councillors had talked about opening a science museum, although not until 1948 did they appoint Mr N. W Bertenshaw, an expert on early engineering, as the director of a potential establishment. Staff were taken on and a core of a collection was ready for display, but where should the museum be? Searching for a site, eyes fastened on the empty Elkington factory. There could have been no better choice. The building was close to the city centre, it had echoed to the clamour of manufacture, and it lay along one of the cuts so influential in Brum's expansion.

In 1951 the first galleries of the Museum of Science and Industry were opened in Elkington's old showrooms. Two years later a former workshop was transformed into the Engineering Hall and the public could now see exhibits which operated. This became a captivating feature of the museum, the involvement of visitors with the machinery on show. From the beginning it was realised that science and technology had to grab the attention of children and adults alike - and the best way to do this was to let them see machinery moving.

Soon the museum began to be filled with significant things from the past. There was a drop forge donated by A. and F. Parkes of Dartmouth Street, makers of shovels and edge tools, a gas engine

manufactured by the noted Smethwick firm of Tangye; a button-shank machine by Ralph Heaton - whose family started the Birmingham Mint; and various machines from elsewhere in Britain and Europe.

Yet there's no doubt about the pride of the Museum of Science and Industry – one of James Watt's inventions. In 1778 the great Scots thinker was approached by the Birmingham Canal Company. When their cut reached Smethwick it had to go through locks to get it over high ground - but the water which dropped into the locks had to be returned to the top of the system. Watt devised a pump engine, installed in 1779 at a cost of £2,000.

Scores of thousands of us have been fascinated by the exhibits at our Science Museum. Soon it is to close. Let's hope that its successor is as popular. And let's hope that the Newhall Street Site will have a grand plaque proclaiming that this was where Elkington's workers astounded the world.

A Spitfire from Castle Bromwich RAF Station being delivered to the Museum of Science and Industry, 17 November 1958. Built by Morris but operated by Vickers, during the Second World War the Castle Bromwich Shadow Factory was the main centre of production for Spitfires in the United Kingdom. Its workers turned out 320 machines in a month to make over 11,000 in total. The Battle of Britain could not have been won without these planes made in Brum. The nearby airfield was the base for the renowned pilot, Alex Henshaw, who tested the machines made at Castle Bromwich.

A MOOCH DOWN THE SHOPS

BREAD OF LIFE

It's knocking off time. The factory gates are opened and a torrent of workers seems to rush from within the great, smoking building. Waiting for them are huddles of children. With a shawl borrowed from their moms and pulled around their little shoulders, older wenches of ten and eleven stand poignantly, holding the hands of the little un's. In over-sized, handed-down jackets, donkey-fringed bigger lads shuffle about in the cold, one eye fixed on the babbies. Most of the kids are barefoot, others wear Birmingham Daily Mail boots. Each of them makes the same plea to the tired grafters.

"'Ave y'any bread, please sir? 'Ave y'any bread, please miss?" Poor and hungry, they seek the bread left over from the workers' butties. Bread. The staple food of the Brummie working class.

How many lads have run a quire of Mails through the streets, selling them to make a ha'penny? With that coin clasped tight in their hands, they've shot down to Mountford's eating house in the Bull Ring so as to buy a ha'penny dip - a piece of bread dipped in the fat of a side of beef roasting in the window. How many moms and dads were frazzled with worry about where the next meal would come from? And how many times were their kids called over by a good hearted neighbour.

Mr Wright, a baker for T. H. Baines of Langton Road, Saltley is standing on the left, about 1930. Sadly he died just two years later. T. H. Baines had a number of shops in East Birmingham. (Thanks to Mrs B. Rose, born Wright).

Ken Mabbett delivering bread for Wilson's of Great Barr Street, Bordesley, about 1956. His van is parked in Ledsam Street, Ladywood, close to Deeley's the greengrocers. Look at all those eggs in the window! (Thanks to Trevor Mabbett).

"Ea'are, son. Ea'are wench, here's a piece for you!"

A piece could mean only one thing - a slice of bread, perhaps covered with lard or dripping. A piece was so much. Because bread was the stuff of life. No wonder that the bakers of Old Brum were so crucial to survival. And no wonder that these men had a passion about making bread, aware that the fruit of their labours meant survival for so many people.

A baker's day began well into the night, with the making of the dough. Flour had been delivered early the previous morning by men strong enough to carry the 140lb bags. It was mixed with water, yeast, fat and salt - sometimes by machines with blades, sometimes strenuously by hand in a trough.

When the dough was ready, it was cut up and measured into 1lb or 2lb weights. Then it was allowed to ferment, after which it was taken out and knocked into the shape of the loaf. Deftly, swiftly and expertly, the bakers manipulated the palms of their hands and moulded the dough into longer lengths to make bloomers. Or else they formed two balls, placed one above the other, dipped their thumb into the top part, scored the dough with 35 cuts and made the distinctive cottage loaf.

There was time to let the dough rest a little, before putting the potential loaves onto a peel - a long wooden handle with a board at the end. Then the loaves were thrust into coke-fired steam ovens. What a tantalising melding of smells wafted out from the bakehouse! There was the powerful whiff of yeast

fermenting - almost alcoholic in its intensity - the full-bodied aroma of dough, and the warm, mouth-watering, scent of bread baking.

Every other street seemed to have its own bakery - with a wall heated by the ovens and so favoured by courting couples. There was West's (later Trippas's) on the Ladypool Road and Duggins (later Greenaway's) of Studley Street. There was Rowland's of New John Street West, Rutters and Abbey's - both of Summer Lane - Slade's of Mary Street, Balsall Heath, and Perrigo's of Belgrave Road. Most of Birmingham's big name bakeries have gone but one of the city's bakers, Starkeys, of Bristol Street, remains. Started in 1888 the bakery carries on the traditions of the Old Brum bakers - the toast of the city.

John Slade, baker of 77, Mary Street, Balsall Heath, the day before he retired aged 91, 10 July 1969. He'd learned his trade as a master baker at the old Cobden Hotel in town and after the First World War he and his wife, Laura, had opened up a small business in Aston. In the mid 1920s they moved to Mary Street where they stayed. His daughters used to earn their 6d a week pocket money by getting down on their knees and scrubbing the bakery floor. Until he retired, John would get up between 4.30 and 6.30 to start work. In this photo he is holding a peel – a wooden, spade-shaped tool used to lay out the loaves in his two-tier oven.
(Information thanks to Dorothy Slade).

DOWN THE LOCAL

Sunday morning - by far the best part of the week. The only morning when he daynt have to get up for work and the only morning when he could do exactly what he wanted. No wonder he sat there, relaxed and contented, in the one proper chair in that little room which was the hub of the family.

He'd had a bit of a lie in, come down and had a saunter down to the paper shop. He'd got his *News of the World* and bought some twist - that thick black lump of tobacco which he took cuts from and mixed with his Bondsman to put in his pipe. He'd come home, had some breakfast and a cup of tea and settled back to read while the kids were larking about outside.

All the while his wife was busying herself, cooking and cleaning up, making sure she didn't disturb the old man. Then he looked at the clock on the mantlepiece and she knew it was time to boil some water. A couple of minutes later he got up and filled the bowl. Stripped to the waist he had a good swill, almost pounding the bar of Sunlight as he washed himself. When he was finished he poured some fresh hot water into his mug, got his lather stick and went over to the mirror on the sideboard to shave himself with his cut-throat razor.

A crowd of regulars outside the 'Vine Inn', a Holt's pub, in Willis Street, Ashted, about 1913. On the corner of Francis Street, the 'Vine' was a beer house and did not sell spirits or wine. Its landlord was Ted Rooke, who ran the pub with his wife Florence.
(Thanks to Doris Reynolds, born Rooke).

Teddy Beedon (left) and Freddy Field having a half of mild in the bar of the 'Gate Inn', Studley Street. Sparkbrook, 1930s. (Thanks to Lil Nead).

Then he went upstairs and put on his suit trousers, his collarless shirt, his waistcoat and his jacket. Back down again, he tied his best muffler about his neck, checked the time on his turnip - the fob watch which hung from his waistcoat pocket – and at exactly five to twelve he put on his billycock. His wife had to have a little smirk. It was the same routine week in week out. She knew what was to come next. He looked at her and said, "What d'y think? Alright?" and without waiting for an answer he was off with a "Tara a bit".

Down the street he strolled, nodding to all and sundry, patting the heads of the kids, doffing his bowler to the women - for all the world as if he was the Duke of the Manor. Then he was there, just as the gaffer was opening the doors. He joined the little knot of his mates and in he went. He never used the snug, always the bar. And he had his own pitch - and God help anyone who dared to stand where he did.

"Alright, Alf", went the barmaid, "What y'having?" As if she never knew! All his life he'd drunk halves of mild and there was no chance he'd ever change. She pulled back the pump and swiftly filled

the small glass with the dark beer, making sure there was a good bit of froth on it. His wife often joked that he loved his ale s'much that he even had to have a head on his tea when he drunk it!

He took a swig and as he did so he turned, putting his back against the pub wall and settling his right elbow on the bar. That way he could survey all that went on. He worn't one for darts or dominoes or even cribbage - although now and then he'd have a game. For him the boozer was where you had a drink, had a yap, had a think, and looked on.

There was nothing like a few halves on a Sunday dinnertime. You were wide awake, not like on a Sat'day night when you were wore out from a week's collar. You'd got a good feed to look forward to, unlike the rest of the week when you were half clammed. You could have a good snooze afterwards. And then on the night you and the old lady would get toffed up and wander down the boozer together.

You could stick the big pubs up the town. You couldn't whack your own local in your own street. That's where you belonged and that's where you was happy. You knew everyone, they knew you. It was where you found out what was going on. It was where you put the world to rights. It was where you celebrated the great events of the nation. And it was where you had the knees-ups and wakes that marked the story of your own family.

The back-street pubs of Old Brum - community centres long before the term was invented.

A sing-song in the 'Benyon Arms', on the corner of Hockley Hill and Farm Street, Hockley. The crowd is mainly Irish lads and their wives belonging to the noted amateur football team Shamrock Rovers. Ned Grogan, their manager from County Dublin, is seated on the left of the piano. (Thanks to Carol Dickinson, Ned Grogan's daughter).

PILLS POTIONS AND EXOTIC BOTTLES: CHEMISTS

It was the most mysterious shop of them all. Not that it was scary. It didn't give you the colly-wobbles or anything like that. Not at all. But it definitely had a touch of secrecy about it, a feeling of the unknown.

Perhaps it was because the door was never left open. Perhaps it was because of the gloomyish look of the place. Perhaps it was because you rarely saw the chemist in his gear outside his shop - unlike the butcher, the baker and the milko.

Or perhaps it was because of all those colourful glass bottles in the window. They didn't exactly brighten the whole place and they didn't get rid of the sense of shadowiness about the chemist's, but they did do their job. No doubt about it, they dragged your eyes to them and to the shop itself. You only had to see them to understand their hypnotic effect. Each bottle was exotically shaped and seemed to

John Blakemore at the entrance to his chemist's shop at 136, High Street, Smethwick, before the First World War. He's advertising Southall's Pure Tablets, photographic plates and teeth extracted! Next door is the baker's of William Woodward and then the tobacconist's and sub-post office of Martha Blomer.

Ronald George Pharo's chemist shop at 404, Monument Road, Ladywood is next door to the paper shop of Thomas Dickens on the corner of King Edward's Road, late 1940s. (Thanks to Johnny Landon).

have been transported to Brummagem from an Arabian tale about Sinbad and the Forty Thieves or Aladdin. The bottom was formed like a large bulb and from this the rest of the glass stretched elegantly and slimly towards a stopper that was pushed into the top. Like great, long decanters they were filled with liquid - and what vivid shades attracted the gaze of onlookers! Some of the vessels were blazing orange, others were bright red, some were deep blue and yet more were thick green.

They were the sign of the true pharmacist, the man who sold not only patent medicines but also his own concoctions. What an important role such chemists had in the days when there was no National Health Service and when even the most good-hearted doctor was costly. If you were poorly then in the first place your mom or gran tried out their own remedies - or else they'd get help from one of the street's wise old women. But if their potions didn't have any effect then the place to go for advice was the chemist with the brilliant bottles.

Inside the shop the walls were lined with shelves filled with the medicines, tablets, lozenges, drops and balms made by the well-known national firms. There were Carter's Liver Pills for backache, Finegan's Nip a Kofs, Sloane's Liniment for muscle pains, Wiz-Woz the King of all pain killers for rheumatism, lumbago and sciatica and Fenning's Powders which had to be taken with a drop of milk on a spoon. Then, of course, there were Beecham's Powders and Beecham's Pills - small pellets of liquorice dusted with a mustard-yellow powder and coming three a penny in a packet of twisted paper.

That wasn't all. Every pharmacist in Birmingham had to sell the Brummie's favourite remedy for drawing splinters and boils. Black, greasy and thick it was crammed into waxed cardboard drums. Its proper name was ungingthamol. No wonder we called it Blackjack! In the same way, the chemists had to stock eucalyptus oil for colds; permanganate of potash crystals for scrages and rashes; and flowers of sulphur for skin complaints.

There were various syrups and linctuses for coughs; allam and iodine for cuts; and a range of solutions to clear out your system – from brimstone and treacle to castor oil, from senna pods to liquid paraffin, from syrup of figs to so many more. And how often has a Brummie kid tripped down to the chemist's chanting 'ippy picky annie wine' so that he or she could remember to fetch some ipecacuanha wine for coughs?

But the real pharmacists always sold their own products as well. With their spotless white coats, starched collars and dickie-bows they were forever ready to lean across the counter and have a private word with someone who had a complaint too delicate to speak aloud. Once they'd got the gist of the problem they'd go into the hidden back room where they had their pestle and mortar, herbs and ingredients and they'd make up a tonic, a pill, a soothing syrup, an ointment or whatever. It might be poppy heads to bring rest to a teething babby, or laudanum to help an old un get some shut-eye. It might be camphorated oil to drip into an ear that was aching or special little cakes to swallow to get rid of worms. And not to worry if you hadn't got a proper bottle for medicines, just bring in any glass container so long as it was clean, empty and could be sealed.

There were so many of these well-respected and well-needed pharmacists, men like Herbert Allen of Summer Lane and William Richards of Mary Street, Balsall Heath. There was Fred Adams of Pigott Street, William Cole of Stratford Road, Sparkhill, Percy Collis of Bournbrook, William Ellison of Villa Road, Handsworth – the list goes on. The Chemists of Old Brum – soothing the sick and succouring the poor.

Shelley's the chemist is on the right at 323, Coventry Road – with the 'Coach and Horses' pub on one side and Ernest Higginson the tobacconist on the other, 1955. Over the road folk are crossing Green Lane, with Jay's the furnishers almost on the corner.
(Thanks to Johnny Landon).

SPIRIT OF CO-OPERATION

It's June 23rd 1881 and it's a fine summer's evening. As the sun loses its strength, a number of railwaymen make their way to a coffee house in Great Francis Street, Duddeston. Most of them work either at the Saltley Sheds or at the Lawley Street Goods Station. They've all got fairly good jobs and they're in regular employment but they're not flush and they're looking for a way to save money and to help each other.

Once they're all gathered, the talk turns to the idea of setting up a co-operative society. They're not the first Brummies to have thought of such a move. In 1828 a tobacconist called William Pare had been influential in starting the first Birmingham Co-operative. It had a shop where members could buy groceries but within a short time the society had disappeared. Yet the idea of co-operation did not go away, and in the 1850s and 1860s a number of other societies started, did well for a few years and then failed.

The blokes in Vauxhall were determined that this wouldn't happen to them. They weren't going to run before they would walk. No, they were going to start in a modest way and do things slowly yet surely. So they elected a chairman, a treasurer, a secretary and twelve other committee members and they

Cutting meat at the butcher's department, Birmingham Co-operative Society, Vauxhall, ready to supply co-op shops across the city, 15 May 1957.

There were many highly-regarded milkmen who delivered for the Birmingham Co-operative Society – but one of the best loved was Albert 'Juddy' Judd. From Arthur Street in Small Heath, Albert was a proper Brummie and proud of it. Here he is with his son David and his well remembered horse, Benita, 1950s. Juddy was a great story-teller and had a saying for every occasion. He often declared that the greatest thing a man could do was to raise flowers in his garden – have children. Rest in peace, Juddy your flowers still bloom. (Thanks to Albert Judd).

agreed to 80 rules. Calling themselves the Birmingham Industrial Co-operative Society, they stated that their objective was to carry on the trade of general dealers and manufacturers of any article of clothing so dealt in.

These pioneers didn't leave things at that. They had meetings and gave out hand-bills to advertise their society and to appeal for new members. Soon they were ready to do business. They rented a shop at 14 Great Francis Street and set about fitting it out with bacon hooks, scales, blinds, letter files, two wooden spoons for ladling jam and treacle, a sugar mallet and chopper, and a table.

Then, on Friday, August 5, 1881, the premises were opened for business. Although the undertaking was small it was a great success and before Christmas a branch was opened at 17 Adderley Park Road, Saltley. The attractions of the Co-op were simple. Customers bought good-quality products at a reasonable price – an important feature when some shopkeepers were still selling watered-down milk and other adulterated foodstuffs. And then, of course, there was the appeal of the 'divi'. Once the Co-op had paid its bills, profits were distributed amongst its customers, each dividend depending upon the sum spent.

The Birmingham Co-operative Society did well and by 1885 it had moved from its little premises and had taken over four shops nearby on the corner of Great Francis Street and Newdegate Street. This

was the beginning of a rapid and spectacular expansion. By the late 1920s there were scores of branches in almost every part of Brum from Witton Lodge Road, Perry Common to Fox Hollies Road, Acocks Green and from Lodge Road, Winson Green to the Alum Rock Road. There were even BCS shops in Coleshill, Oldbury, Smethwick, Solihull and West Bromwich.

But the society was more than a retailer. It had a boot repairing factory in Great Francis Street; coal wharves in Witton, Stechford, Harborne and elsewhere; and a laundry in Holyhead Road, Handsworth. There was a bakery and a garage for delivery vehicles in Great Brook Street, a confectionary department in Adderley Road, and a bacon curing plant and a dairy in Vauxhall Road. The society even had its own farm in Lea Marston.

Each branch was recognisable because of its large plate glass windows the slogans which proclaimed 'BCS – Only Best', and the way in which the word 'Co-operative' was written like a signature above each shop. The branches were vital to the success of the Co-op and many of them were large – just like that on the Coventry Road which had ten shops and a hall.

The biggest and grandest store of all was the Central Premises in High Street, Birmingham, opposite New Street. Opened in 1916 it had seven stories which housed a gents' outfitters, a restaurant, grocery shop, departments for drapery, tailoring, furnishing and boots and shoes, and administrative rooms. Ten years later the Grand Louvre drapery across the way was taken over and the Co-op proudly bestrode both sides of the High Street. Like so many other businesses, the Co-op has faced difficulties recently and the Central Premises are no more. But the Co-op itself remains, a major enterprise founded in Old Brum by working men who wanted to co-operate with each other.

The High Street premises of the Birmingham Co-operative Society, during a winter in the late 1970s.

TRADING PLACES:
THE BULL RING

The youngster looked up intently with his eyes fastened firmly upon his mom. "Hold on tight to me donny, and don't let goo! D'y'ere me, ma lad! There's loads of people about and I don't want you wandering off and getting lost. I've got lots to do and I can do without you getting me all mithered."

He nodded his little head ever so slowly at every word she said. Seeing him so serious, she couldn't help but soften. With a hint of a smile glancing across her mouth and a sparkle glinting through her eyes, she made it up to him. "And if y're good, I might buy y' an ice cream an' we'll pop into the Market Hall and let y' stroke the puppies and kittens."

That swung it. There was no way he was going to allow his little hand to be pulled from his mom's clasp, for all the bobbing and weaving she did to get them through the crowds and down High Street from the tram stop.

As they turned the bend just beyond the tiny Scotland Passage, it seemed as if a torrent of folk were pouring down the hill, pulled by a great yet unseen magnet towards the spire of St Martin's. He wanted to stop and catch his breath, but he had no chance for his mom was lugging at his arms. Looking sharply

Two preachers on a stand in the Bull Ring, probably early 1900s.

A cracking view of a bustling Bull Ring, packed with traders and shoppers, 4 December 1954. The sellers of food are tight against the statue of Nelson, whilst a variety of 'swag merchants' line the pavements of Spiceal Street, going down towards Jamaica Row.

right and left, she dragged him quickly across the horse road to the mighty Market Hall, fronted by it's two huge columns. Below lay the Bull Ring, a triangular-shaped piece of land that seemed to start at Nelson's Statue and end at the darkly bricked church.

He knew what it was like 'cus his dad sometimes brought him up town on a Sunday when it was quieter and you could look about. Often, they'd stand on the edge of a crowd around one of the preachers. Then off they'd mooch to listen to the different speakers going on about politics and harking at the hecklers.

But Saturdays in the Bull Ring were different. It wasn't just busier, it was heaving with shoppers – and not just from Brum, for there were plenty of folk from the Black Country and Worcestershire. And the atmosphere was also different. It was hectic, exciting and loud.

As his mom ducked and dived along, he had no real idea what was going on. All he copped sight of was close-ups of coats and frocks, swallow raincoats and jackets, ganseys and jerkins. As for the cobblestones, he knew they were there, but they were carpeted with a tightly-knit and forever moving pattern of pumps, hob-nailed boots and shoes.

If there were few views, what evocative noises fought to gain his attention. Over there was an old lady almost wailing "andy carriers, andy carriers", as she sought to flog her home-made brown bags. Nearby, was an elderly chap whose voice raspingly told folk of the benefits of buying his Old Moore's Almanac. And just beyond, another feller temptingly called youngsters to part with their coppers for his coloured beads.

Then there were the flower ladies, holding out a bunch of blooms to the shoppers, pushing their faces forward and calling out the prices. Best of all were the cries of the barrow boys who were strung out from Bell Street down Spiceal Street and into Jamaica Row. Yells of "apples" and "taters" and roars of "Ee are, c'mon on then. Look at this lot. Y'wunt get better. Y'wunt get cheaper. Come on ladies!"

It was a real education, finding out that people had so many different sounds and tones to their voices. Some cajoled, others urged; some almost pleaded, others seemed to order; whilst others explained, teased or bantered.

As the afternoon beckoned the early evening, it became easier to take notice of what was going on. Hard by Lord Nelson, the escapologist was trying to get out of his chains, the fire-eater was swallowing flames and quacks were striving to offload their patent medicines.

Near them were a few maimed men playing mouth organs or dulcimers. His mom always flung a bit of silver into the cap of one of them, telling her son they'd fought for their country and that they should never be forgotten.

They never should be. Nor should all those characters who made Brummagem's Bull Ring.

Louie Chapman and Joe Caffrey laying a wreath 'In memory of the Old Bull Ring from the stallholders' at Nelson's Statue, 12 September 1959.